Myrna L
The Film Qu   s

1

"A smile can change everything. It's something I always try to bring to others."

Copyright © 2023 by Dustin Alan Daniels
All rights reserved.

The content of this book may not be reproduced, duplicated, or transmitted without the author's or publisher's express written permission. Under no circumstances will the publisher or author be held liable or legally responsible for any damages, reparation, or monetary loss caused by the information contained in this book, whether directly or indirectly.

Legal Notice:
This publication is copyrighted. It is strictly for personal use only. You may not change, distribute, sell, use, quote, or paraphrase any part of this book without the author's or publisher's permission.

Disclaimer Notice:
Please keep in mind that the information in this document is only for educational and entertainment purposes. Every effort has been made to present accurate, up-to-date, reliable, and comprehensive information. There are no express or implied warranties. Readers understand that the author is not providing legal, financial, medical, or professional advice. This book's content was compiled from a variety of sources. Please seek the advice of a licensed professional before attempting any of the techniques described in this book. By reading this document, the reader agrees that the author is not liable for any direct or indirect losses incurred as a result of using the information contained within this document, including, but not limited to, errors, omissions, or inaccuracies.

CONTENTS

1. THE DEBUTANTE (1905-1918)

2. THE BACCHANTE (1918-1925)

3. THE PERFECT WIFE (1931-1935)

4. THE QUEEN OF THE MOVIES (1936-1942)

1. THE DEBUTANTE (1905-1918)

In Montana, we refer to them as ranches, but they are also farms. Everything is grown here. For a young youngster, the ranch was a great location. Wild flowers with their delicate scent grew all over the front fence. The foothills were covered in bitterroot, a type of cactus with lovely violet blossoms, but they were a pain if your horse stomped on them. Since this is plains country, Grandmother Williams hadn't planted any flowers. Of course, she still had apple trees in the backyard, and my grandfather had cottonwood trees planted all around the home. Cottonwood, they taste nice and are really attractive. I used to taste all of the flowers and leaves.

Mother claims that I used to get butted by my baby lambs and that I frequently dozed off all over my cats, Timothy and Alfalfa, in my high chair. They were given their names by my father in honor of the grasses that were used as cattle fodder. A rancher valued these things highly. My legs could hardly fit over my darling old dobbin, Dolly, because she was so large. However, I continued to ride her without a saddle and only a bridle while donning a ten-gallon hat that was larger than I was.

In those days, there was always music even if there were no radios, phonographs, or traveling orchestras. Uncle Fred played the guitar, Mother and her sister Lulu Belle, my Aunt Lou, both played the piano and the violin, and we had a German ranch worker who was a skilled violinist. They would play me to sleep with the Berceuse from Jocelyn and Brahms's Lullaby out in Montana where there isn't supposed to be any culture, gathered around the piano in the parlor with other musical friends and family.

Back then, we had two active ranches: one for wheat and one for livestock. My father, though, never fully returned to ranching after his time in the capital. When I was five, he lost interest in the plan and we relocated back to Helena. For some reason, he didn't go back into politics, instead turning to real estate, becoming a bank director, and dabbling in stocks and bonds. He was simply amazing; he resembled Santa Claus and always descended the hill with his arms laden with gifts. He made a huge deal out of holidays, especially Christmas, which was wonderful and filled him with joy with its festivities—stories, decorations, gifts, and food. Because Mother abhorred cooking, he always prepared the holiday feasts. Having learnt how to do it around a campfire during roundup, he was also rather excellent at it. He actually developed into quite the gourmet for a cowboy, bringing us cracked crab on ice all the way from Chicago. What a sweetheart he was, so generous.

On Fifth Avenue, which was obviously not Fifth Avenue, New York, we enjoyed the high life. It was simply a lovely middle-class area. On the other mountainside, the majority of the wealthier families were developing. We had magnificent, steep streets because Helena is a large city that rises up Mount Ascension and Mount Helena from Last Chance Gulch. When it snowed, you could slide all the way to the railroad station in the town's valley area past Judge Cooper's residence. Just below us, in a moderately opulent home with an iron fence surrounding it, the Cooper family resided. My parents knew them, but I didn't spend much time with their four years older son Gary, who attended school for a while in England. We used to make fun of living on the wrong side of town in Hollywood, but oddly, we hardly ever brought up our time in Helena. That didn't stop him from discussing them with others. Gary would enthusiastically describe me as "belly bustin' hell-bent for election" as I walked past his house down the street, according to Edith Goetz, Louis B. Mayer's daughter.

William Powell, Myrna's former co-star, stated that Gary Cooper had disclosed that she had vivid red hair in braids, large freckles, and a turned-up nose after the three met in Hollywood. She wasn't particularly attractive, but something about her appealed to him. Both of them were bashful, and the only thing he enjoyed most about his courtship was sitting on the Williamses' picket fence while Myrna played "The Wedding of the Winds."

When he visited the Williamses' home one afternoon to run an errand for his mother, it was the only time he ever spoke to her during those Helena days. Myrna was directed to the cellar for a drink of apple jelly by Mrs. Williams, the epitome of Montana hospitality. There was a dark pit behind the furnace that Myrna had developed a fear of. She fearlessly descended the stairs and cautiously made her way to the jelly shelf, but sights horrifying and foul emanated from the black hole. Myrna screamed "Yo-oo-oow!" as she tumbled up the cellar stairs, injuring her knees and ripping her stockings.

The most ungallant thing Gary Cooper ever said to a woman was probably when he stated, "You're a sissy," as Master Cooper put it. There have undoubtedly not been any complaints since. Completely embarrassed, Myrna made the hasty decision to immediately forget the entire incident, including Judge Cooper's young son. Eventually, they crossed again in Hollywood, but Myrna had already descended into the weeds and Gary was preoccupied with the volatile Lupe Velez. The romance between Loy and Cooper never materialized.

John G. Brown, Jr., a different neighbor, was my first love. He wasn't actually my beau, though. He had no time for me despite the fact that I had a huge crush on him. He would allow Ruth Rae, my girlfriend, to ride on the back of his trike while I just followed after, horrified by the whole situation. Ruth would ask me to call him up for her on Saturday afternoons, and I would do it like a fool. He continued doing this for quite some time, but he never once looked at me.

Who should give me my first fan letter years later, when I started working at Warner Brothers? Jonathan Brown He wanted images of me for his college room despite the fact that I had only played a few roles, most likely the Orientals. He said the entire college was interested in learning about me. I suppose this is my payback for all the years he ignored me, I reasoned.

Grandmother Johnson's home in the valley section of the town was where I spent a lot of my childhood. There, she had the most exquisite gardens, complete with pansy beds, peonies, and tiger lilies that were taller than me. I found programs from touring companies that performed at the Marlow with celebrities like Mrs. Fiske and John Drew in her front-hall settle. I was captivated by them for some reason. I would constantly take them out and read through them.

Grandmother would take me to the theater if anything proper was showing, she was wearing her adorable little hat with the velvet pansies. Oh, what a lovely person. She always had excellent taste, and my mother did too. Even with what I was wearing, one play from that era, Maeterlinck's The Blue Bird, definitely stands out. My dress was made of blue China silk, or so they called it back then. It was incredibly delicate. My mother had given me a blue feather fan, which I could use instead of the barrettes in my hair. I must admit that this play, a true spectacle, completely astounded me. I had never witnessed anything more incredible in my life. I'm positive that the Blue Bird was what eventually succeeded in getting me.

We had completed a couple projects in class. I recall wearing a goofy dress and playing some sort of angel in the gym once. My piano and sketching courses, however, had taken priority. In truth, my aunts, who were devout Methodists and Presbyterians, and my art teacher—a nun at the nearby Catholic convent—had made me pretty religious. I went through the typical stage of self-sacrifice where I yearned to be a nun or nurse and live my life serving others. However, anything other than performing on stage felt unthinkable after The Blue Bird. Being a nun was far more honorable, but it was still appealing. Though the world and the flesh prevailed, it took me a while to come to terms with the thought that I wasn't noble.

In our cellar, where Mother stored jellies and preserves, not on the side of the furnace with the coal chutes and the shadowy area that Gary remembered, I started performing plays. I set up a curtain and declared Sleeping Beauty as my debut performance, making up all the lines but resisted the urge to play the lead. The youngster they used to taunt with "Redhead, gingerbread, five cents a loaf!" had a carrot-topped, freckled face, and wasn't pretty enough to be Sleeping Beauty. I handed the part to a girl who lived up the street who had thick, blond bologna curls, and I was happy to play the prince. I turned my mother's black stockings into tights, donned my black bloomers over them, and constructed a collar out of paper in the style of Sir Walter Raleigh. The centerpiece of my outfit was my mother's exquisitely lovely gray-and-black ostrich plume, which I tucked into one of my father's hats. I invited family, friends, and Johnny Brown to the performance, which was rather brave of me as a generally timid young lady. I knew it would impress him. Oh, my God! Mother shrieked as I entered. My feather is here. I drew the curtain to conclude the show while still stunned. That was my first acting role.

My mother was in danger of passing away from pneumonia in the winter of 1912. Everyone seemed to have given up and there were empty oxygen tanks all over the home when her nurse entered with a full tank and managed to save her life. My father sent us off to La Jolla, California, a beach town close to San Diego, which became a fantastic location for me, so as to spare her the remainder of the winter in Montana. A steep, rocky cove was across the street from the residence we chose. When the tide was out, though, I could descend some roughly hewn cliff steps to collect specimens with my best friend Mr. Kline, who ran the neighborhood aquarium. At high tide, waves would reach the road. Imagine a six-year-old having access to such a superb guide to Hell's Bottom's abundant aquatic life!

Mother cherished Southern California and recognized its wealth of opportunities. She persuaded my real estate agent father to purchase, among other properties, the Sunset Boulevard corner where Charlie Chaplin would later erect his studio when he came down for my seventh birthday. At that time, it had nothing on it. Although my father was "a Montana boy, by God!" he could have made a mint. He has no plans to visit California. He exclaimed, "Enough!" at last, and we all went home. There was a lot of conflict surrounding that. I now see that Mother was feeling the difficulties of a strong woman who is unable to do what she wants to. She participated in local politics and was actively interested in her music; he was a Teddy Roosevelt Republican; but anything more than that would likely pose a danger to my father's position as the family's head of household. Mother wasn't a pushy person who put others under pressure, but she opposed all forms of nationalism and prejudice. She was not snobbish or prejudiced.

I recall the arrival of the first black family in our area. In 1912, there weren't many black people in Helena, and the other residents were either suspicious or worse. Mother did not differentiate at all. She greeted them and invited us to interact with their kids. One Sunday morning, she yelled from the front porch, "Myrna, come look at this." Isn't that wonderful? The young black boy from across the street, Bubby, was wearing play clothes while my little brother David, a towhead, was sitting on the sidewalk next to him. He was dressed for church in a starched linen suit. The contrast and closeness of those two young boys left me with a happy recollection that I've treasured my entire life.

There was a lot of tension between my parents. My dad wished for his family to live in Montana. California was where my mother wished to live. She suggested that it would be safer to have a hysterectomy in Los Angeles because she required one. He eventually caved, so my mother, David, and I left once more. We initially resided with her friend Viva McLaughlin in Ocean Park on Hart Avenue while mother recovered before moving across the street into our own home. Our home featured two stories, shingles, a sun porch with a swing, and trellises covered in tiny pink Cecile Brunner roses, much like all the other homes on Hart Avenue. There was honeysuckle growing everywhere. It was a tranquil place to be in Ocean Park. In that beachside neighborhood, making friends was simple, and there didn't seem to be much violence or crime. We did experience a scandal, though. Two boys were detained for playing marbles for money but were released into their parents' custody.

Three streets away from Hart Avenue, which led to the ocean, was the Nat C. Goodwin Pier, complete with a cheerful café and a thumping orchestra. The first jazz was being played at the time, which was before World War I. Mother traveled there with friends from Montana or neighbors from Ocean Park who were frequently seen in the area. She found this aspect of life appealing—parties, clubs, champagne, and music. She was a very homosexual woman who loved life a lot.

Barnacles and invertebrates that cling to the pilings under the pier were my favorites. A private beach next to the pier and my first movie stars were the results of my explorations. They were dressed in lovely bathing suits with their hair styled in turbans like Valeska Suratt. Of fact, everyone had to swim in stockings and some form of bloomers back then, but the people in the movies just appeared more glamorous. They seemed to be something incredibly sophisticated. They would chase us away when we tried to observe them covertly beneath the pier. While taking a tour of Universal Studios, where a Western was being produced, I got a better look at movie actors. I always recall the blue lights—they didn't have white lights back then—and William Farnum shooting it up with some wranglers when I gaze up at that hill. I found the whole thing fascinating, but I had no plans to stop going to the theater.

The girl next door, who I had never met, sent over a balloon when I was bedridden for a few days due to a cold or another illness. She went by the married name of Louella Bamberger and remains one of my closest pals.

A few days after mailing the balloon, Lou MacFarlane recalls, "I was coming home from school when a lovely, lilting voice, which she had even then, came from behind me saying, "Excuse me, aren't you the girl who sent me the balloon?" I looked back and saw what appeared to be a goddess. She was at least three feet taller than I was. I was ashamed to send the balloon because Myrna reached her full height at a young age—she was eleven when we met, but I was eight—and I thought she looked more like a young lady.

Since we both had younger siblings, we started taking them to the beach, where we would construct sand castles and make up tales about what happened within. On the next block, we developed crushes on two boys. I mean, I was old enough to not care, but Myrna had a thing for the lads. I would have a crush on the other, slightly tougher lad; if Myrna wanted to have a crush on whatever the name of the elder boy was—he was Russian, extremely exquisite, and very handsome—that was great. We made them the heroes of our sandcastle stories, which were heavily influenced by the Saturday serials, because we were too young to otherwise be interested in them.

Every Saturday, we went to the cinema, but the only movie I can ever recall seeing is The Perils of Pauline. We would then proceed to the Ocean Park pier's ballroom, where kids could dance on Saturday afternoons. Myrna offered to teach me to dance even though I had never done it before, saying, "It's easy; I'll teach you." Myrna would lead and I would follow as we entered the ballroom, where she would teach me how to dance.

I think dancing affected me. I started acting like what I had seen on stage after draping Cecile Brunner roses around my ankles and in my hair. How I persevered! Although I didn't begin taking lessons until we returned to Montana, I was a natural dancer. At that point, my father once more put a stop to things and exclaimed, "You're coming home!"

America was undecided about intervening in Europe's war, and the Williams family was at odds over potential presidential candidates. While my father tended to favor Charles Evans Hughes and intervention, my mother fought for Woodrow Wilson and peace. My family taught me about politics early on, from a variety of perspectives. I was not raised to be intimidated; voicing one's thoughts is part of being an American. They thought it was your right and obligation to participate. Both my father and my uncle Arthur were legislators in Montana. Mother actively participated in Democratic groups, while Aunt Lou held the position of Broadwater County Treasurer. In 1916, I was drawn to Wilson's advocacy of "peace without victory" and the League of Nations. My mother and I persuaded my father to choose Wilson over Hughes on those points.

My grammar school teacher was an elderly, rigid woman who had also taught my mother, and we had more everyday issues. Although my weakest subject was mathematics, her area of expertise—her true love—I was eager to pass her big test. I went to my father's sister, Nettie's husband, Uncle Len Qualls, a teacher, and he helped me prepare for the test. That woman accused me of cheating when I passed. Since my father was known as "Honest Dave," it was obvious that honesty was important in our family. It was unimaginable to cheat. I left the room after complaining about the teacher to the principal and left for home. And I wouldn't return until she expressed regret!

To offset the risks of grammar school, at least there were dancing lessons. Miss Alice Thompson, who chose me to appear in the Rose

Dream Operetta at the Marlow Theater, had just begun teaching me ballet. These events used to be organized by a man by the name of Jansen, who donated the proceeds to civic organizations like the Elks. It was a significant occasion in Helena. I created my own dance routine, which was naturally inspired by The Blue Bird, and I also created a stunning diaphanous blue costume. Grandmother Johnson passed away the previous year, leaving a dreadful vacuum in my life; I just wish she could have seen it. Nevertheless, my mother was thrilled and proud, but my father left town for work the day before the performance. He might have done it on purpose to show his disapproval of my theatrical aspirations. For him, every performance was burlesque. Even though it, along with my first review, was on the society page, he must have seen the large photograph of me in costume that appeared in the local newspaper.

Wilson was elected, yet we still started "the war to end all wars." My dad considered joining the military. He had to be hurt, in my opinion. He was having issues, maybe some I wasn't aware of, but mostly the ongoing conflict between him and Mother was having a negative impact. Looking back, I sometimes believe he was most likely experiencing a breakdown. His decision to enter the war at the age of 39 was borderline suicidal.

He informed me he would surely enlist one warm autumn night while we were sitting together on the back porch. "You're my little soldier," he declared. I was donning a child's military uniform, a jacket that seemed like it belonged to a soldier, and a small headgear. "When I leave, I'm leaving you in charge. It might not last very long. Perhaps it will. But your father will rely on you. You'll always look after your mother and brother if I don't return, won't you?

That occurred in the autumn of 1918, soon before Helena was hit by the Spanish flu. The town was destroyed. Nobody could provide nurses. Doctors were impossible to find; at most, you could convince them to drop by before they vanished into the night. People traversed the streets covering their mouths with improvised surgical masks. David and Mother both contracted it. They were nursed by my dad and me. It dawned on me once they were partially recovered. My father set up a couch in the dining room for me because I couldn't be upstairs with the others. He looked after all of us, even me. He used to come and wrap me in freezing sheets every night in an effort to lower my body temperature. I can still picture that man sitting directly over me as he endured my misery with me out of fear that I could pass away.

When I finally got through the difficulty, Mother and David both recovered. One night, as my father slept upstairs in his room, I was still in bed downstairs and heard horrific noises. He was leaking blood. Because he had been so preoccupied with taking care of everyone else, he most likely had this sickness for a long time before it manifested. and in particular, looking out for me. So, I started to cry. They took me across town to one of my mother's acquaintances, a woman who had stayed with us in California, to get me out of the way. She owned a large, three or four story house. I simply moved from room to room.

There is a proverb in Swedish that claims someone will perish if a bird flies into a window. Well, as I was exploring the house, a bird struck one of the windows in the parlor as I was entering it. A short while later, the phone rang, and I immediately started sprinting up the stairs as quickly as I could. They began calling me, but I remained unresponsive. When I eventually walked downstairs, Mother's friend was sobbing on her bed. My dad had passed away, I knew.

Ironically, he passed away as the population was celebrating the fake armistice, which was announced in the press before the Germans officially signed it. On November 11, 1918, the actual armistice day, we interred him at Forestvale, a cemetery outside of town. When we arrived back at Helena, she was enraged. People cheered while standing in the streets. Firecrackers exploded and sirens sounded. A parade with torches that night wound its way through the city. The party lasted for two days and could be heard from our house of mourning up the hill.

You see, I completely worshiped him. I overcame his loss by taking on the duty he had given me to care for my mother and brother. Years passed before I realized the extent of the harm this had caused.

I became the one who had to look after them as a result of it. In actuality, too much and for a very long time. I waited till I was over 30 before getting married. When I told an analyst about it years later, she responded, "What a terrible burden to place on a child!"

I objected, "But I wasn't a child. I had reached adulthood. It, of course, was completely false. Just recently, I turned thirteen.

2. THE BACCHANTE (1918-1925)

While mother adored Montana, she didn't enjoy the harsh winters. She considered going back to California following the passing of my father. Her close friend from Ocean Park, Viva McLaughlin, had relocated there. Why not visit Culver City if you do come, she said in her letter. Then we did. California is always fantastic when you first go there, so of course when we moved there I thought the same thing.

Between Hollywood and the Pacific Ocean, in the hamlet of Culver City, we purchased a home on Delmas Terrace. We had fruit-bearing peach, apricot, and miniature orange trees in our garden. Over the driveway, trellises arced, packed with rose bushes that were four or five times larger than those found in Montana's wildflower meadows. In the back, we kept a goat. Goat's milk was recommended for my brother who had TB-like symptoms. It appears that the goat's milk was effective because the TB vanished quickly.

I used to instruct Sunday school at the Presbyterian church when we first got here. I once failed to hear Mr. O'Connell, the clergyman, respond to a biblical question. He covered me in fire and brimstone. I didn't return. When I was dancing between the two huge palm trees in the front yard, my mother was concerned that he may notice me. There, I organized dance performances alongside my Ocean Park coworker Lou MacFarlane and Jean Vandyke, a Mississippi girl whose brother was an actor. We performed Ruth St. Denis positions a la "The Water Lily" across the front lawn while donning homemade Grecian tunics.

Earlier—at the time, it was just Goldwyn—Metro-Goldwyn-Mayer was located in Culver City. There were a good number of studios. Thomas H. Ince's had a liveried black butler who welcomed invited guests at the door, giving the impression that it was a Southern estate. There, Hal Roach operated a studio for many years. There might have been a few additional tiny fly-by-night locations, but those were the main studios. We would scale the fence and enter the Goldwyn rear lot even though they were off-limits unless we had official business. We would pose for photos while dancing on top of the fence and holding positions while seated on the standing sets. We had fantastic ideas. With the studio and the dance company, I was going to portray Ruth St. Denis, and Lou would compose the plays for us to choreograph. She invented the tales that my sister and I secretly acted out on the Goldwyn back lot when we were children. Later, when the situation was drastically different, I would go back there.

I attended the Westlake School for Girls in Los Angeles because of my mother. That had been settled in Helena because wealthy brewers named Kessler, whom she knew, were sending their two daughters. She didn't pick that incredibly exclusive institution because it was exclusive—Mother was never in the least bit snobby—but rather because it promised to support my artistic endeavors. She did not have much money. In Montana, perhaps, my father's legacy would have been adequate, but not in California, not to Mother's tastes. She taught private music lessons and assisted at a friend's clothes business to supplement her income. There, she used to buy clothes for me. I was undoubtedly the finest dressed girl at Westlake, while not being the richest.

I traveled to work on the Venice Short Line, which ran all the way from Western Avenue to the ocean. We had fantastic streetcars, and I wish we still had them. After getting off at Western Avenue and moving a few blocks to Westmoreland, I would arrive at Westlake. My time there got off to a good start thanks to a particular music teacher who came in to teach me piano and a beloved language instructor. They had a May Festival, where I could dance. I took private ballet lessons at Mme. Matildita's École de Choreographic Classicet in downtown Los Angeles. I cherished those afternoons in the city. I used to go to the public library after class and pick out a bunch of classics to read on the Venice Short Line ride home.

Former La Scala ballerina and star Mme. Matildita taught all the postures in French and used traditional European methods, slapping you if you moved improperly. I couldn't dance on my toes, which is my tragedy in terms of ballet, she revealed. They lasted for too long. Toes that are fairly stubby and short are ideal because they will bend under. Dancers' feet already suffer through hell, but mine were simply useless. "Never, never, will you dance on those toes!" Madame ruled. The lessons, however, were a rewarding experience and the foundation for everything I achieved after that.

Large windows encircled a sort of ballroom where classes were held on the top floor of the Majestic Building. One day during class, the building trembled and the entire room began to shake. As is typical of my response to such occurrences, I halted and stood still. Others sprinted furiously, seeking to board the elevators that had stopped moving. However, Madame had been in the earthquake in San Francisco. Where there is probably a steel girder to hold if the walls collapse, she stood in the doorway. The walls remained. I believe the center hit Long Beach, sparing Los Angeles from significant damage. My first earthquake, though, was a real shock. My front yard's two lovely palm trees were uprooted when I finally arrived home. All through the night, Culver City experienced aftershocks. They went on forever. Oh, my God, this will never end, I kept saying as I gazed out the window.

On Delmas Terrace, we had amassed a sizable ménage. Old Sederburg, the Radersburg-born partner of Grandfather Johnson, stayed with us. He was a bachelor who had always resided with our family in Radersburg until moving in with my grandmother in Helena and then, after she passed away, either with my aunt or with us. He kept a sweetheart hidden away, and when he passed away, she received his sizable estate.

Aunt Lou Wilder, Mother's sister, whose late husband had worked as a dentist in Townsend, as well as my cousin, moved in with us. One day as she was crossing the street with her daughter Laura Belle, Laura Belle merely fell, and from that point on, she was unable to walk by herself. She undoubtedly had an illness that causes muscle deterioration, but these disorders are now curable. If they had known then, we might have been able to help her, but we were only able to offer comfort as she lost strength.

Aunt Lou found refuge in Culver City, and my mother was spared of the chores she detested—cleaning the house. Mother was a shrewd woman; she always found a cook to help out. Although she was good at some of her specialties, she generally detested cooking. My aunt was an excellent cook who also loved to do it. I profited from having Aunt Lou present in a number of ways. She and I were quite close. She gave me a lot of the domestic necessities that my mother did not.

Mother was a very active woman who became president of the Culver City Women's Club and was heavily involved in the arts. She played a key role in the founding of the Hollywood Bowl along with her dear friend Bessie Zuckerman, another vivacious woman. They had a close relationship with L.E. Behymer, the Philharmonic's impresario, who brought all the touring shows and concert performers to Los Angeles. He was yet another musician friend of Mother's. I was extremely lucky to be able to take part in her artistic circle of friends.

Later, I met Barry Jones and Maurice Colbourne, two English performers, at one of Bessie's banquets. They pleaded with me to accompany them on their tour with a Shaw repertory group. They said, "We're going to kidnap you." "You are the ideal Shaw woman," I said. That was the environment I grew up in, and my mother had a big part in it. She must have been quite frustrated by the fact that her music was never used. If she hadn't had two children and lived when she did, she most likely would have been a concert pianist. I'm not sure. It's difficult to say.

Misses Vance and Delaguna, who were in charge, called me into the office during my second year at Westlake. They started accusingly, "We understand that you are taking dancing lessons downtown."
Of course, I replied, "Yes." I've been dancing at your festivals, haven't I?
"Oh, yes, of course," was the response. See, they were having trouble with this. What are your plans for it, then?
I informed them, "I intend to do it as a professional." "I want to be a great dancer," said the speaker.
"Well! This is awful, I tell you!" They were in awe. What happened next escapes me, other than the sense that, even at that young age, this was a mindset toward the theater. You see, such institutions were only created in those times to turn us into "ladies." I had already

studied table etiquette and all of that at home. They weren't things I had to learn in school.

In addition to socializing with artists at home, Mr. Behymer brought top actors and musical performers to the Philharmonic Auditorium, where we held season tickets. I observed Duse. I heard Paderewski, Gigli, Galli-Curci, and Chaliapin. There, when I was a small girl, I saw Pavlova. She performed The Dying Swan, a unique piece that Fokine, I suppose, choreographed. It was not Swan Lake. She is shot by an arrow, and as I recall, there are small splatters of blood on the feathers. The most heartbreaking and stunning thing I had ever witnessed was her dying. Over the years, I've observed others do it and pondered, "What's wrong?" There is an omission. How did she act? Then I understood what it was—the pounding of my heart. Pavlova made a tiny but incredibly touching gesture over her breast to show the heartbeat. Until she passed away, it beat a little bit slower after a little bit slower.

So as you can see, I was shocked by the Westlake attitude. I didn't ask those two females, "What am I supposed to do?" I simply said, "Thank you very much," and left the building.
I went home and told my mum about the entire event. This is terrible, I said to her. "I no longer want to go there." She responded, "Yes, it's terrible, and you shouldn't go there."

The Westlake School for Girls, which is currently located right in the heart of Bel-Air, is dependent upon the young people who were the target of their mockery. When you consider it, it is funny. They were such snobs! In actuality, it was, and to some extent still is, throughout much of Los Angeles for many years. Until they need money for a music center, they always seem to have a negative attitude about the movie industry. I received invitations to social events in Los Angeles, possibly as a result of my mother's connections. Anyhow, Irene Dunne and I were both invited. The only two actresses that were asked to do anything down there were us. They probably mistook us for "ladies"—whatever that is.

I changed from Westlake High School toward the seashore to Venice High School. Ironically, it had a higher degree of cultural engagement than Westlake. Notable individuals from every aspect of the arts came to meet with us, and concerts were flown in from Los Angeles. My English instructor W.H. Head, sometimes known as "Old Pop Head," taught us to always use a "a" that is somewhere in between flat and broad. That is still one of my most valuable lessons. Despite the fact that my grandparents were from Scotland and Wales, none of their offspring had a British accent. They had no impact on the so-called "Western twang" either, much of which is fake. They were fluent in English. That was confirmed by Pop Head. He also decided that if the senior cast broke her leg, I would play Ophelia in the senior class play. Although the senior didn't break her leg, I had a fantastic opportunity to study Shakespeare as a result. (When Venice High dubbed its yearly speech and theater prizes the "Myrnas," in my honor, I was moved and honored.)

Harry Fielding Winebreiner, a fantastic art teacher at Venice High, inspired me to start sculpting. In reality, I wasn't very good and wasn't good enough to continue, but something unique came out of it. The school's administration made the choice to adorn the fountain in the sizable lily pond in front of it. A girl reading a book, a young male athlete, and, towering above them, a figure signifying youthful aspiration were Mr. Winebreiner's choices for the sculpture group he was commissioned to make. I was the model he picked for "Aspiration."

The ambitious statue needed hours of hard posing with its arms extended and head up. To create the flowing look of the curtains, he covered my torso with damp fabric and gauze. Once it was completed, a local promoter named Bert Lennon—father of the Lennon sisters—worked it into the city's Memorial Day celebration. I was brought on board the USS Nevada, which was anchored a half mile off Venice, along with a plaster cast of the statue. Under the expert direction of Culver City's first filmmaker, Thomas H. Ince, I came to life on a deck draped next to my plaster likeness. The remainder of the ceremony called for me to scatter flowers from the battle ship's prow. Lord! I thought the whole thing was a mess, yet it received a lot of positive feedback.

The amazing sculptural ensemble endured for fifty years and eventually became famous. The young males have undoubtedly been plagued by "Aspiration," who wears gauzy clothing. They would march to Venice after Santa Monica football games and wrap rubber tires around her neck and arms. They were always modifying the statue in some way, but nothing significant. But now, vandals have gotten their hands on it. It's inhumane! In fact, they knocked my head off!

I was a dance instructor at the Ritter School of Expression in Culver City while I was a student at Venice High. Even though my students were virtually toddlers and didn't dance much, we still managed to teach them something. My mother received my $40 monthly salary directly from Mrs. Ritter. I also filled in as a splicer at the Hal Roach Studio for a friend. The film had already been chopped, so all I had to do to join the pieces was feed them into a machine and pull a lever. I don't recall the image, but I believe a dog was in it. Because it was the first time I had been paid personally, my paycheck stood out more. Around eighteen dollars for the week looked like a huge sum of money.

During that time, mother frequently visited Montana because she had maintained strong ties there. On my eighteenth birthday, we were split up since I was typically too busy to go with her. She sent a telegraph from Helena, which I still have. She is extremely typical in this regard: I miss myrna. you reach maturity today. Let's pretend you feel ages. If I were there, what a celebration it would be. When I get home, I'll have one. cousins and brother auntie uncles join in love and best wishes. mother.

My obsession with dancing, if not on my toes then at least in the contemporary forms of St. Denis and Duncan, led me to continue taking dance and music courses. I wrote lists labeled "Literary Characters to be Interpreted in Dance" and "Emotional Qualities to be Expressed in Terpsichorean Form" in notebooks in abundance. Rupert Brooke, Rachmaninoff, and Rabindranath Tagore were among the poets and composers I mentioned as favorites. I adapted these works for recitals at the Ebell Club and other cultural organizations, persuading Lou MacFarlane and Betty Black to skip class so they could perform with me. Whenever I recall what I did! I have no idea how I managed it, but that period of time in my life was excellent overall. I've had a great life for the most part.

Having stayed in touch with Lou, I was introduced to Betty Berger, who is now Betty Black. She became one of my closest friends, and she and Lou became excellent buddies. You know, being able to retain people is a beautiful thing. It's not always easy to hold onto people—you can keep some, you can't keep others. Betty and Lou had to be very patient with me later when I started getting into movies. But they persisted. They've had to put up with a lot because, at least for me, when you work in movies, you just don't do anything else. I value those relationships.

In Venice, the junior high school was right adjacent to the high school, and I remember leaving one day with Lou. There, this tall girl was awaiting a streetcar. She welcomed Lou enthusiastically, and Lou introduced her by saying, "Betty, this is Myrna Williams that I was telling you about." When I did eventually meet her, I was ecstatic. We were below her as she stood in the sunlight on an incline. When I turned to face her, I noticed her bright red hair and freckled, turned-up nose. She had a lovely, soft voice, and while she spoke to Lou, I was struck by how beautifully her long fingers moved. This girl with the tiny turned-up nose captured my attention.

Lou and I were included in the invitation Lou's mother extended to Myrna's young pals. Teenagers from Culver City began to congregate at their residence, with Myrna serving as sort of the center of the wheel. She had gained popularity on the Venice High campus.

She was selected as the school's most attractive and talented girl—sort of the May Queen—for the May Day exercises that year after Mr. Winebreiner had completed her statue.

Under Myrna's influence, the majority of the people who visited the house developed an interest in dance. As a result, she established a small dancing school where she taught us modern dance and pantomime and wrote plays for us to perform. To be able to sit up and watch the dancing, her cousin Laura Belle would wait all day for us to arrive. Laura Belle was really attractive in my opinion. However, I found everything about Myrna to be lovely. Myrna's mother would prepare something special called "shrimp wiggle" after we had finished dancing. Because Auntie was obsessed with Laura Belle at the time, she actually prepared meals. Della truly went above and above to make this the hub for both her creative son and her daughter. She got involved in their endeavors because she wanted them to have the best of everything, which she thought should have included their pals.

In the summer of 1923, about that time, Myrna started seeking legitimate work. We were informed that Grauman's Egyptian Theatre in Hollywood had a few openings. She submitted an application to join the chorus of the previous films' live prologues. We all patiently waited by the phone to learn if Myrna had been accepted because there were hundreds of girls who applied.

I dropped out of school when I was eighteen. I needed to. At the time, not being able to graduate was a terrible tragedy, but I had to work since money was getting low. "Myrna, go to work!" was not said. I believe it was the sense of accountability my father had instilled in me. I don't mean to be a martyr; I think it was exciting to be able to continue dancing.

I went to a Los Angeles audition location to try out for Fanchon and Marco. Sister and brother were a dance team that found great popularity performing prologues for national theater tours. They paid me $35 every week, which was pretty good money back then. It undoubtedly boosted household finances.

The Egyptian was an upscale movie theater, just as stunning as the Chinese that Sid Grauman later constructed. This live prologue concept was developed by Grauman, who was the first person to exhibit movies in style. He had a renown for his prologues and was already considered a Hollywood icon. He wasn't someone I knew when I worked there. He was a deity; when you first start out, everyone important is a god. If you're a punk, you don't know your producer. All that we did was dance.

Twelve years later, when he requested Bill Powell and me to leave our footprints in the Chinese Theatre's forecourt, I had a new perspective on him. Bill and I made the decision to have some fun because Sid was rumored to be a fantastic practical joker. We wore big clown shoes that were at least a foot long when we showed up for the ceremony. I won't ever forget Sid Grauman's look, though. We nearly hurt his feelings. He took great pride in that routine and couldn't stand the thought that we were making fun of it. It was really difficult for us to persuade him that it was a joke. "To Sid, who gave me my first job," I wrote when I had put my mark in the cement, which helped to reassure him.

In the prologue of the first Ten Commandments film by De Mille, I began at the Egyptian. Fanchon and Marco were exceptional dancers and demanding bosses. According to the form, everything had to be quite strict. We practiced all those Egyptian-inspired square movements since the dance was meant to accompany the Biblical scenes in the film. We wore tiny slacks, halter-style headdresses, and a type of Egyptian halter. I was informed it was quite fascinating and reportedly fairly lovely.

I can't recall any horrific trauma related to my first working experience. For whatever reason, I can't recall, but I know we were all incredibly terrified. Naturally, my mother visited me and gave her approval. Even if she didn't think it was amazing and it couldn't compare to the style of dancing she was used to, she nevertheless supported my involvement in all aspects of the arts because she was a huge admirer herself. She continued to see to it that I was given tickets to the plays that Mr. Behymer imported.

I took my partner in the dance, Lillian Butterfield, to watch Duse. We were only able to see the final acts of the three plays because of our matinées at Grauman's. Everything was set up in our dressing room so we could change and board the streetcar to the downtown Philharmonic. On one occasion, the second act of Thy Will Be Done was about to end as we ran into the theater. Duse screamed with such a piercing sound that it really floored me. Even though she could only speak Italian, her heartbreaking wail made it clear that her son had rejected her.

The venue was crowded. We went extremely high to the second balcony, where Mother could only find a few seats. However, we had a fantastic view of the entire stage, which was dominated by a petite, gray-haired woman in her sixties who was absolutely outstanding. Even when she played a young woman, she never wore makeup, but she was utterly captivating. Her dominance was the intriguing aspect, which I must have remembered forever. Duse was quite restrained in her actions, in contrast to Bernhardt, who seemed to overact and show off—aside from, of course, at dramatic moments like the scream.

A woman approached Lillian, who had a dark, Mediterranean appearance, as we stood there sobbing during Duse's curtain calls and said, "Oh, I'm not even Italian like you, but I cried, too." We didn't understand a word she said, and neither did we, but we were all brought to tears. And there, in the middle of a field of red roses, stood Duse, a small woman with gray hair who I will never forget as long as I live.

She resumed her tour and arrived in Pittsburgh two months later. On one wet night, she was unable to enter the theater. I am familiar with that emotion. I've experienced it countless times. You try to find a stage door and you lose it because you can't get in and nothing seems to function. She evidently got wet, developed a chill, and then passed away. In Pittsburgh, Eleonora Duse passed away while on that tour.

At Grauman's, I made several lifelong friends, including Lillian, Melva Lockman, and Helen Virgil. We went out for supper on Hollywood Boulevard in between our matinée and evening performances because we had two shows each day. At that time, it was still fairly pleasant. Hollywood was a tiny community. It still is, however it is now seriously dilapidated. It resembled a small Spanish town more at that time since it was lighter and had an easier quality. There were farmlands and vast fields with California poppies and pepper trees, all of which had a pleasant aroma. Around Egypt was a business district made up of around six blocks of low buildings with predominantly yellow and white paint. Henry's, The Blue Front, and Frank's Café were a few of the good eateries among them where we would eat.

I rented a home close to the theater with Melva, Lillian, and Helen because I was sick of driving four times a day between Culver City and Hollywood. I had never before lived apart from my mother, and it was the first time. Although the house with the females didn't work out, she wasn't overly happy about it because she had made up her mind to keep her brood near the nest. I eventually took on the role of the mother, cooking and cleaning everything, so I left and returned to Culver City. But throughout the years, I stayed acquainted with those girls.

I used to visit Myrna on the weekends when she lived in Culver City again, Betty Black recalls. I once took the streetcar to her house after school to demonstrate the type of relationship we had. I was sitting there with my books and long, dark locks when a woman next to me remarked, "You're certainly a pretty young lady." I was around sixteen years old and as green as grass. She approached me and began interrogating me. She patted my knee and announced, "I'm going to Hollywood." Why don't you accompany me to Hollywood? She kept patting my leg and becoming more forceful. I was frightened even if she were a lady. She was sort of holding me somewhat when I grabbed my books, leaped off the train, and sprinted all the way to Myrna's.

We went to bed early because Myrna arrived home from Grauman's pretty late and had an early rehearsal call the next morning. I couldn't wait to share my strange experience with her. When I told Myrna the incident, I said, "Wasn't it ridiculous of me to be so afraid? She merely wanted to be kind and take me out for tea. Simply put, I didn't enjoy how she grew nearer to me.

Myrna said, "Well, Betty, you knew instinctively that something was wrong. "At your age, you must use caution. You see, you can have affairs with people other than males. Women are capable of having affairs with other women.

But how were they able to achieve it? How do they act?
"Well, at Grauman's, we've talked a little about it, though I'm not familiar with all the techniques. You were extremely clever to act as you did because you don't tend to do that kind of thing.

My mother had not given me any information about the realities of life, and my family was all orthodox Orthodox Jews. Until the day I got married, whenever something frightened me, didn't seem right, or seemed kosher, I would go to Myrna. I had assumed that others would just make fun of me, but she would explain. She always carefully described it, even though she was a teenager—she was eighteen at the time.

When a group of girls was present, we would stay up late at night talking about various topics. She had concerns about politics and world issues even back then, which other children might have found a little odd. Prudence was not something she valued. She had no interest in the conservative females at our school or the girls who thought very practically. She was usually drawn to those who were pursuing their interests. Even in those days, she thought that strict moral standards and social mores were archaic Victorian. Now we say that. Myrna had been repeating that when she was fifteen and sixteen. Her perspective was far ahead of its time.

I was confused and guilty when Bob Black asked me to marry him since a rabbi had made me swear on my father's grave that I would never wed a gentile. Myrna was aware of our relationship and had high hopes for Bob. She explained, "They preyed on your emotions when your father passed away. "You can't berate yourself for making that commitment. Forget superstitions if you want to marry Bob and you believe it is the correct decision for you. I eloped with Bob after she got me a gorgeous nightgown for my huge trousseau. From the time I was thirteen years old till... until now, sixty years later, she has had an impact on me.

My second prologue included an East Indian nautch dance before Douglas Fairbanks' The Thief of Bagdad. We had bells on our ankles, whirling skirts, and no shoes on us. That belonged to me. I found that appealing. Actually, we probably were belly dancers at the time, but we weren't aware of it. In any case, it was enjoyable to perform with all those beautiful moves and bare feet. Throughout my early years in Hollywood, I frequently wore my bare feet.

The Fanchon and Marco ballets were occasionally used by producers in their films. For an orgy scene in The Wanderer, a Raoul Walsh film based on the Prodigal Son parable, they hired the Thief of Bagdad cast. So, to play bacchantes, we all went to Paramount. That comes to mind because I was trying to follow their instructions while acting ridiculously, drinking, and leaning over this couch with a wine goblet. I wasn't particularly impressed with the filmmaking overall. Movies weren't a novelty in Culver City because of all the studios there. There were many professionals who worked in the film industry there as well as aspirants from all over who came to attempt. Warner Brothers director James Flood lived directly across the street from us. There were several Metro players and techs nearby. Truman Vandyke, a Selig-Roark serial actor, was a relative of mine. He used to take me tea dancing at the Montmartre on Hollywood Boulevard, a popular hangout for celebrities. However, I wasn't interested in the movies. I used to dance.

They performed in Egypt for several months. They made the decision to hang some photos of the dancers in the courtyard after ticket sales for The Thief of Bagdad started to decline. Henry Waxman, a well-known portrait photographer, was coming to choose girls for the pictures, our stage manager announced. He picked me, Helen, and Melva. He first took pictures of the other girls at his studio on Sunset. He then began attacking me. He lost his mind. All night long, he simply continued taking pictures—long shots, close-ups, portraits, and art studies. I couldn't move throughout the matinée the following day due to exhaustion.

When Rudolph Valentino arrived for a sitting, Henry had several of my photographs blown up and displayed throughout his studio. What's her name? Valentin enquired. Henry explained, "She's a little girl from Grauman's I found the other night. "Isn't she amazing?" You know, Henry was so enthralled by my beauty that he took my picture. Valentino seemed to concur. He enquired, "Could she come over to the studio?" My wife should see her, I want.

Natacha Rambova, his wife, had essentially moved into his place of work. Their first independent production, Cobra, required a leading actress, so they went seeking for one. She and I met at the Ritz-Carlton Productions offices in Paramount. She was the most stunningly beautiful woman I had ever seen. When her mother wed the perfume manufacturer, Winifred Shaunessy—her real name—became Hudnut. Natacha Rambova, her own creation, was a better fit. She consistently wore turbans and very long, stark outfits, usually made of the same golden brown velvet or brocade as her eyes. I was terrified even though she was gorgeous.

To reassure me, she said, "I know people call me everything from Messalina to a heroin fiend, but I truly don't eat little dancers for breakfast. She offered to bring some of her clothes for me to wear because she wanted to do a test and assumed I was a helpless young child. She ignored my worries when I expressed concern over a slight gap between my front teeth by saying, "Oh, that can be fixed. We can just cover them with hats.

Valentino was constantly around, but I didn't pass the test with him. He had a fantastic appearance, more resembling a panther than a manly jungle beast. I simply lost my mind. Imagine! He was a huge star when I was a child, but he was never in the spotlight, which pleased me because I was so little. I thought he was a very kind man who was personable and seemed well-bred. He was also far less showy than his wife. He never did any of that "sheik" crap, just like I never did any "exotica" with him later. Valentino was a kind Italian man who enjoyed working on automobiles. That was how the "Great Lover" passed his time, driving his collection of unique vehicles about.

I borrowed Rudy's mobile changing room so I could get ready for my test. He showed up as I was getting ready with a rabbit's foot, which was used back then to remove powder in place of a sable brush. He stood there talking briefly and then, "I thought maybe you could use this," hoping to soothe my nerves before the test. He inquired, "Have you got everything you need?" and turned to leave, saying, "You look perfectly lovely." What a sweet guy!

It was simple to understand why Natacha decided to manage his career. He agreed to everything and then expected her to save him, acting like a gullible youngster who only wanted to be liked. Rudy's wife was made out to be the bad guy because everyone knew how nice and accommodating he was. After they split up, she insisted, "I was a fool, young, idealistic, and full of fight. I was unaware of the futility. Studios don't give a damn about you or your ideas. They want to take as many photos of you in as short a time as they can to learn as much about you as possible. What occurs to the star is unimportant. It would be some time before I actually experienced the truth of what she said.

I didn't do much in the test; all I did was take a few books, move them across the set, and put them on a shelf. Such a test was conducted in order to obtain various viewpoints. You see, we didn't have sound yet. The Valentinos had set up a screening for me, so I brought Henry Waxman along. There were just the two of us. I had never before seen myself on a screen before. Oh, that was incredible! With me running around with the books, rushing here and there like the Keystone Kops, it appeared to be one of those old wound-up movies. Oh, it was so bad. I couldn't grasp it. I wasn't moving that quickly. Henry was also perplexed. He also had little knowledge about movie projectors. I was really heartbroken when I returned home.

The operator had very carelessly screened the movie at the incorrect pace, it turned out. Being ignorant of such things at the time, I lacked the sense to understand that. In any event, my engagement in Cobra came to an end at that point. The Valentinos didn't call me back; they rightly opted not to use me. Everyone attributed it to Natacha, claiming "Mrs. Valentino didn't like you," but without training, I would never have been able to pull it off. I was still a thin child and simply too young. A girl from M-G-M named Gertrude Olmstead was employed.

My major focus remained dancing, but the Valentino experience greatly piqued my curiosity in movies. Despite my resolve, I would get bored with those prologues because they went on for so long. I was aware of the need to adhere to stringent rules and to travel with the other girls, but on occasion, I would go above and above. The revised prologue for Romola, a play by Lillian Gish, was being practiced when Fanchon said, "Myrna, you need to be in the movies. You constantly strive to achieve something new.

There was nothing in front of me when I made the decision to leave the Egyptian Theatre, which is unusual for me. Nothing. But I had come to the realization that I was going nowhere, and that was not the direction I wanted to continue in. I wanted to venture out and do something, possibly visit New York. That departure choice strikes out clearly. Everyone was in disbelief. "What are you going to do?" they all questioned.

I did more of the Denishawn stuff while dancing at events; it was really spiritual. In addition to receiving a stirring poem titled "To a Danseuse" from a retired U.S. Army major, I also won a Gothic-style medallion from the Norse Studio! I frequented the Metro-Goldwyn-Mayer casting office in Culver City, which was located right next to the studio's main entrance. I used to go there and sit down on a wooden bench there every day. Aunt Lou would comment, "I don't know how she does it." I'd go crazy. I lack the patience necessary to carry out what she is doing.

Bob McIntyre, the casting director, sometimes known as "the god in the grille," noticed me one day in late 1924. "You all right?" he enquired. Have you eaten enough? Naturally, I lived nearby where there was plenty to eat, but he hired me nevertheless because I appeared so despondent: "Look, we're making a test of Kathleen Key's costume, the leper outfit, for Ben-Hur. Put off applying makeup. Just go to the stage so-and-so and get the dress.

My first opportunity to enter M-G-M's gates. I was thrilled. I hurried down to the set while wearing the leper costume after going up and donning heavy stage makeup. The makeup artist, Lillian Rosine, looked at me and said, "My God! Where did you purchase that cosmetics from? Without seeking permission, she grabbed me and lifted me back up while applying decent makeup. (She treated all of us like children; she was always like that.) When she lowered me once more, I had garnered a little attention. I was approached by Christy Cabanne, who was in charge of one of the Ben-Hur sections.

He inquired, "Are you under contract here?"
In a contract? No! I just entered. I've been attempting to enter this location for a while. After they completed the outfit test at the end of the day, he returned, but I had no idea what he was getting at.
He said to me, "I'd want to try you for the Virgin Mary in Ben-Hur. We search the area but cannot locate anyone. Rosine was summoned and instructed to get Rosine a gorgeous blonde wig.

They put me through a test the following day, which, from what I hear, was fantastic. I never understood why they kept it there for years and would pull it out and exhibit it around Christmas, but it must have been extremely spiritual. Regardless, it caused a huge rift between two studio factions: Was the actress supposed to be a famous person or a complete unknown? They thought about the danger of employing a stranger who would thereafter develop a "reputation." Everything was foolish and stupid. I believed that they would research my sex life, which I didn't have much of at the time because I was so young. The groups who desired me and those that desired a name competed with one another.

Bob McIntyre gave me a $7.50 per day side job in the interim. I portrayed one of several mistresses encircling a Roman senator in his box at the races while Rosine covered my red hair with a heavy, black wig dripping with pearls; a far cry from the Virgin Mary. On the rear lot where the gigantic Circus Maximus set had been constructed, that historic chariot race was filmed. As I waited for them to begin, a black limousine pulled up, and out emerged a small blonde woman who had several people circling her. At the time, I was unaware of who she was, but I soon did. They hired Betty Bronson, who had recently performed as Peter Pan at Paramount, for the role of the Virgin Mary. I think they believed Peter Pan would keep them safe.

I received a job in Pretty Ladies as a consolation gift from Bob McIntyre. I first met Joan Crawford at that time. In this production, which starred ZaSu Pitts, Tom Moore, Norma Shearer, Conrad

Nagel, and several people dressed as Ziegfeld Follies performers, we were both chorus girls. It's incredible to imagine that Norma, Joan, and I would eventually all play significant roles for M-G-M. And there we were—Joan and I, these two insignificant auxiliary figures—working as a human chandelier. With our toes sticking out and all these gals moving in different directions, they had us clinging onto this object. A riot broke out.

Joan had recently signed a contract and was surviving solely on black coffee in order to look thinner for the camera. Back then, she was still Lucille Le Sueur. After Pretty Ladies, they held a contest to come up with a new moniker for her. Oh, she was amazing! She urged me to go down to the Ambassador and dance with her while she was learning all the new dances, including Charleston and Black Bottom. Of course, being a dance snob, I wouldn't want to participate. But it was Our Dancing Daughters that ultimately made her a star.

One day, Joan entered the changing room and was very upset. She stumbled onto my lap, crying as we both became marabou snowflakes that kept falling into our lips. Joan suffered from severe anxiety. Although I never expressed it, I did. Harry Rapf, the producer who found her, reportedly chased her around the desk the previous evening. Her situation was miserable. They were all vying for her because of her stunning body. I didn't have all that much trouble, but my somewhat snobbish demeanor turned them off.

The best thing that came out of my first M-G-M encounter was becoming friends with Joan, and we have remained friends ever since. I wasn't signed by them. Nobody took any action to keep me despite the hype surrounding my Ben-Hur test and Pretty Ladies. Later, I returned and essentially lived the remainder of my life there. Then, however, they didn't grasp me.

To the rescue came Natacha Rambova. I quickly arrived at the studio after Henry Waxman called to let me know she needed me there. When I called home to tell Lou and Betty that Natacha had recruited me for a small but prominent role in What Price Beauty, they waited by the phone. My friends from Grauman's, Lillian Butterfield and

Melva Lockman, joined us for a celebration after Mother prepared a midnight meal. Five of us slept crosswise in one double bed while they stayed the night, chatting and making grand plans for our futures.

What Does Beauty Cost? had a terrible writing that used a Rambova twist on the country girl in the big city subject. She had discovered a talented young designer named Adrian Greenberg, from whom M-G-M's Adrian originated. His main scene, which was also my only appearance, was a futuristic dream sequence showing many kinds of women. I was referred to by Natacha as "the intellectual type of vampire without race, creed, or country." Adrian created a stunning set of red velvet pajamas for me, complete with a very, very snaky short blond wig that ended in tiny points on my forehead. Three years passed before this odd movie was produced, but Henry Waxman still snapped photos of me wearing that dress. They surfaced in a fanzine with the headline "Who is she?" and ultimately resulted in my first contract.

I once went with a group of young artists who, if we had been in New York, would have lived in Greenwich Village—writers, painters, sculptors, and would-be writers. Williams was thought to be too common by some of them for a performer. I objected. It seemed like a perfectly good name to me. They started throwing about variations, horrible combos, and very stupid names after mentioning Earle Williams, Kathlyn Williams, and a few more actors by that name. Even worse, someone even proposed the play on the Mona Lisa, "Myrna Lisa," which I thought was uncomfortable. Then a crazy Russian free verse poet named Peter Rurick unexpectedly came up with "Myrna Loy." I then asked, "What's that?" I thought it sounded fine, but I wasn't yet persuaded to change my name.

Of course, my Welsh pals have never been persuaded. Richard Burton would never introduce me by that name, despite the many years I spent as Loy. He would always ask, "Do you know Miss Williams?" whenever we went somewhere. Same goes with Emlyn Williams. They viewed my altering it as a serious offense. Well, I suppose that is, but back in 1925, when Henry Waxman had shot those photographs for What Price Beauty?, I had written "Myrna

Loy" on the back. They were delivered to Minna Wallis, the ruler at Warner Brothers, by that wonderful man who was always pitching me.

My first opportunity to enter M-G-M's gates. I was thrilled. I hurried down to the set while wearing the leper costume after going up and donning heavy stage makeup. The makeup artist, Lillian Rosine, looked at me and said, "My God! Where did you purchase that cosmetics from? Without seeking permission, she grabbed me and lifted me back up while applying decent makeup. (She treated all of us like children; she was always like that.) When she lowered me once more, I had garnered a little attention. I was approached by Christy Cabanne, who was in charge of one of the Ben-Hur sections.

He inquired, "Are you under contract here?"
In a contract? No! I just entered. I've been attempting to enter this location for a while. After they completed the outfit test at the end of the day, he returned, but I had no idea what he was getting at.
He said to me, "I'd want to try you for the Virgin Mary in Ben-Hur. We search the area but cannot locate anyone. Rosine was summoned and instructed to get Rosine a gorgeous blonde wig.

They put me through a test the following day, which, from what I hear, was fantastic. I never understood why they kept it there for years and would pull it out and exhibit it around Christmas, but it must have been extremely spiritual. Regardless, it caused a huge rift between two studio factions: Was the actress supposed to be a famous person or a complete unknown? They thought about the danger of employing a stranger who would thereafter develop a "reputation." Everything was foolish and stupid. I believed that they would research my sex life, which I didn't have much of at the time because I was so young. The groups who desired me and those that desired a name competed with one another.

Bob McIntyre gave me a $7.50 per day side job in the interim. I portrayed one of several mistresses encircling a Roman senator in his box at the races while Rosine covered my red hair with a heavy, black wig dripping with pearls; a far cry from the Virgin Mary. On the rear lot where the gigantic Circus Maximus set had been constructed, that historic chariot race was filmed. As I waited for them to begin, a black limousine pulled up, and out emerged a small blonde woman who had several people circling her. At the time, I was unaware of who she was, but I soon did. They hired Betty Bronson, who had recently performed as Peter Pan at Paramount, for the role of the Virgin Mary. I think they believed Peter Pan would keep them safe.

I received a job in Pretty Ladies as a consolation gift from Bob McIntyre. I first met Joan Crawford at that time. In this production, which starred ZaSu Pitts, Tom Moore, Norma Shearer, Conrad Nagel, and several people dressed as Ziegfeld Follies performers, we were both chorus girls. It's incredible to imagine that Norma, Joan, and I would eventually all play significant roles for M-G-M. And there we were—Joan and I, these two insignificant auxiliary figures—working as a human chandelier. With our toes sticking out and all these gals moving in different directions, they had us clinging onto this object. A riot broke out.

Joan had recently signed a contract and was surviving solely on black coffee in order to look thinner for the camera. Back then, she was still Lucille Le Sueur. After Pretty Ladies, they held a contest to come up with a new moniker for her. Oh, she was amazing! She urged me to go down to the Ambassador and dance with her while she was learning all the new dances, including Charleston and Black Bottom. Of course, being a dance snob, I wouldn't want to participate. But it was Our Dancing Daughters that ultimately made her a star.

One day, Joan entered the changing room and was very upset. She stumbled onto my lap, crying as we both became marabou snowflakes that kept falling into our lips. Joan suffered from severe anxiety. Although I never expressed it, I did. Harry Rapf, the producer who found her, reportedly chased her around the desk the previous evening. Her situation was miserable. They were all vying for her because of her stunning body. I didn't have all that much trouble, but my somewhat snobbish demeanor turned them off.

The best thing that came out of my first M-G-M encounter was becoming friends with Joan, and we have remained friends ever since. I wasn't signed by them. Nobody took any action to keep me despite the hype surrounding my Ben-Hur test and Pretty Ladies. Later, I returned and essentially lived the remainder of my life there. Then, however, they didn't grasp me.

To the rescue came Natacha Rambova. I quickly arrived at the studio after Henry Waxman called to let me know she needed me there. When I called home to tell Lou and Betty that Natacha had recruited me for a small but prominent role in What Price Beauty, they waited by the phone. My friends from Grauman's, Lillian Butterfield and Melva Lockman, joined us for a celebration after Mother prepared a midnight meal. Five of us slept crosswise in one double bed while they stayed the night, chatting and making grand plans for our futures.

What Does Beauty Cost? had a terrible writing that used a Rambova twist on the country girl in the big city subject. She had discovered a talented young designer named Adrian Greenberg, from whom M-G-M's Adrian originated. His main scene, which was also my only appearance, was a futuristic dream sequence showing many kinds of women. I was referred to by Natacha as "the intellectual type of vampire without race, creed, or country." Adrian created a stunning set of red velvet pajamas for me, complete with a very, very snaky short blond wig that ended in tiny points on my forehead. Three years passed before this odd movie was produced, but Henry Waxman still snapped photos of me wearing that dress. They surfaced in a fanzine with the headline "Who is she?" and ultimately resulted in my first contract.

I once went with a group of young artists who, if we had been in New York, would have lived in Greenwich Village—writers, painters, sculptors, and would-be writers. Williams was thought to be too common by some of them for a performer. I objected. It seemed like a perfectly good name to me. They started throwing about variations, horrible combos, and very stupid names after mentioning Earle Williams, Kathlyn Williams, and a few more actors by that name. Even worse, someone even proposed the play on the Mona

Lisa, "Myrna Lisa," which I thought was uncomfortable. Then a crazy Russian free verse poet named Peter Rurick unexpectedly came up with "Myrna Loy." I then asked, "What's that?" I thought it sounded fine, but I wasn't yet persuaded to change my name.

Of course, my Welsh pals have never been persuaded. Richard Burton would never introduce me by that name, despite the many years I spent as Loy. He would always ask, "Do you know Miss Williams?" whenever we went somewhere. Same goes with Emlyn Williams. They viewed my altering it as a serious offense. Well, I suppose that is, but back in 1925, when Henry Waxman had shot those photographs for What Price Beauty?, I had written "Myrna Loy" on the back. They were delivered to Minna Wallis, the ruler at Warner Brothers, by that wonderful man who was always pitching me.

3. THE PERFECT WIFE (1931-1935)

I wasn't really found by anyone. Every time a director or producer noticed a characteristic he could bring out that I frequently wasn't even aware I have, I was repeatedly discovered. My introduction to M-G-M by Irving Thalberg was a surprise to me at first. But it turned out that even he wanted me for a really peculiar role: the cruel trapeze star in Freaks who marries a midget for his money and then poisons him. Almighty God! Thalberg too! That is how challenging it was to get rid of that thought.

So, I was spared by fate from freaks. Baclanova understood it, but there was no better option. Metro introduced me to a series of rather unremarkable, undoubtedly insignificant ingénues. It didn't feel like growth to be portraying a spoilt snot who mistreats Marie Dressier after six years and sixty photographs. I'm sure my displeasure was evident. "Get your chin up, kid," Marie said. "The entire world is ahead of you," Emma was entertaining because of her. She was delightful, a wonderful woman, full of life, and compassionate. I had an obsession with her. With her strong presence and amazing accomplishments, she also exuded awe. When she was in her sixties, she had almost completely disappeared and had come back, becoming the biggest box office attraction in cinema history. She seemed to go on and on forever.

I was required to take three shots simultaneously while rushing from set to set. I would don a blonde wig after finishing a sequence for Emma and do a scene with Jimmy Durante for The Wet Parade. He would inquire, "Moyna, where'd you get that schnozzola?" Jimmy was always intrigued by my nose. I would then take off the wig for a sequence with Robert Young in New Morals for Old. When I just ran into him outside of Universal, we laughed once more at one of his movie lines. Do you still recall what I had to say to you? Bob queried. "I want to run my bare feet through your hair," you say?" I was saved by Rouben Mamoulian, who used me in his musical parody of Lubitsch called Love Me Tonight. Rouben was one of my beaus, so I knew him. We weren't engaged in any significant activities, but we were close friends and occasionally went on dates.

Now pay attention, Myrna; this is what's going on. The Countess Valentine is crucial to my vision for the movie, but Paramount is adamant about getting rid of her character. Although she won't be in the screenplay, I already know what I'm going to do with her. For as long as they don't view it my way, I'll send your lines separately. Rouben was someone I trusted, so I said, "Sure, I'll try anything!" He would mail short pieces of blue interoffice memo paper with four or five lines of text every few days. On my end, this was. When the men in the front office saw my first scenes, they replied, "Oh, yes, keep her." I have no idea how Rouben did it.

Lou MacFarlane claims that Myrna's charming off-hand delivery of those sentences is what made them so painfully humorous. Despite having a minor role, she stood out, and Jeanette MacDonald unintentionally increased her prominence. In a gown that wasn't all that different from MacDonald's, Myrna arrived on the set for a masquerade sequence looking even more stunning, but Miss MacDonald declared, "I want that dress."

They gave Mamoulian Myrna's outfit, so I assume she didn't want any trouble.
I hurried down to the wardrobe section with Myrna to get another one. After a dreadful time sifting through yards of costumes, we eventually found a delightfully simple black velvet outfit that was probably worn a thousand times before. Although it seemed to be little, Myrna looked stunning after donning it and adding a few small tucks here and there. You didn't see anyone else in that scene until she arrived back onto the set wearing her black dress and powdered wig. You see, everyone else was dressed in pastels, such as whites and pinks. And that person, whose name I can't recall since she looked like such a horrible person in the photograph, was furious. She was unable to declare, "I want that dress!" Never in my life have I witnessed somebody so enraged. Therefore, Myrna might not have had such an impact and been a star if she had not worn the pink outfit that MacDonald appropriated. The future?

Adore me Tonight served as a showcase for Maurice Chevalier, the main musical star of Paramount. I would be picked up by his automobile and driven to the San Fernando Valley, where we would film some hunt scenes. I recall having just brief interactions with him while we were driving in the mornings. After watching his vivacious on-screen appearances, I anticipated a vibrant individual. However, he was one of those persons with extreme restraint, something like Hank Fonda. He continued to be a mystery to me, Chevalier, a very weird man who kept to himself entirely. Then he would enter the scene, the lights would turn on, and this amazing moment would take place that everyone adored.

When we finally connected on the summer circuit almost forty years later, I finally understood it. I wrote a message letting him know that I could make it to his final performance because I had Barefoot in the Park rehearsals during the day and he played at night. Ladies and gentlemen, he said, "I am going to sing a song in her honor from a picture we made together a long, long time ago. An old friend of mine is in the audience tonight." After singing "Mimi," he invited me to stand with him on stage. The moment he kissed me, the entire house erupted in screams and shouts while Maurice exuded warmth and charm in spades. The following day, there was discussion about Maurice Chevalier kissing me in all the quaint stores in and around Cohasset. The women were agitated. And when dad was well into his sixties, I finally saw the personality I had always expected from him.

Before he left, we took a few photos together, and I requested him to sign one of them and mail it to me—something I hardly ever done throughout my whole career. You don't consider those things when working with people. If I did the same, Maurice promised to send one. We then traded autographed photos.
That day, he informed me, "I'm going around the world one more time; one last tour and then I'll take it easy.
"I don't believe it," I remarked. But after that tour, he did retire, and not long after that, he passed away. His life was lived on stage.

Oh, Love Me Tonight is rich! Do you have any idea what we had in that movie? The writing was punctuated by Charlie Ruggles and Charlie Butterworth, and Maurice and Jeanette MacDonald sang the beautiful Rodgers and Hart songs "Isn't It Romantic?," "Lover," and "Mimi," in which I even had a verse—the only time I've ever sung in a motion picture. In that picture, Richard Rodgers and I became friends. He enjoyed making fun of Arthur Hornblow. My relationship with Arthur really began at that point. When we first met, his wife had already left him and brought their son to a Beverly-Wilshire pharmacy. Since the previous year's Arrowsmith, we hadn't seen each other. The following day, a gorgeous bouquet of roses and an invitation to supper showed up. Oh, that one did things well! The rest of the time was devoted to Arthur. What did you do over the weekend? asked Dick Rodgers. "Catalina," I exclaimed, perhaps a little too openly, "with Arthur Hornblow." Dick gave me the impression that he was saying, "Oh, brother, she's hooked." Then I was.

That was a pivotal period for me because Arthur and a fresh understanding of my talents both happened at once. Valentine was imagined by Rouben as a pent-up aristocrat who was desperate for life and men and so utterly bored that she would constantly be sleeping—on the staircase, on the furniture, or wherever. When Charlie Ruggles cries, "Valentine, Valentine, could you go for a doctor?" She is dozing off on a tiny Empire sofa at one end of this enormous salon. She instantly perks up and says, "Yes, bring him in!" She is talking about her favorite subject during the hunt scene as usual when Jeanette's character interjects, "Don't you ever think about anything but men?" Valentine responds, "Yes, young men." When you hear them today, they sound like the corniest phrases ever, yet the house was torn apart. The preview audience just yelled, after all. It was at this point that I first realized I had a funny voice or that I could make people laugh. You know, I hadn't realized I could be humorous during any of those sober sections.

When showing Love Me Tonight at the Museum of Modern Art in 1986, Joseph L. Mankiewicz said, "For me, the highlight of the picture was a young actress named Myrna Loy." Myrna was the reason you forgot who acted beside Chevalier because she sang; she was light, lissom, and charming. I believe Myrna got the picture while she got Chevalier.

My humorous abilities being shown by Rouben didn't bother M-G-M. They immediately inserted me back into the vamp stereotype by lending me to RKO for Thirteen Women. As a half-caste Javanese-

Indian, I meticulously kill all the white classmates who have taken advantage of me. I don't remember much about that racist invention, but it was brought up recently when I received the National Board of Review first Career Achievement Award. When I was preoccupied elsewhere, Betty Furness, a charming mistress of ceremonies who had started at RKO, filled in for my hands in close-ups, said that she had been fired from Thirteen Women. There were only twelve in the final print, despite the title. I told her, "You're lucky because I almost murdered you, too. Irene Dunne was the only person in that picture I managed to avoid, and I constantly felt guilty about it.

The villainous daughter of Boris Karloff's title character, Fah Lo See, was cast as me in The Mask of Fu Manchu by Metro. The final straw was indeed that script. In one clip, she ties this handsome young man up before whipping him and making gleefully provocative noises. I had been reading Freud, but it seems the authors hadn't. I told Hunt Stromberg, our producer, "I can't do this." "I've done some awful things in movies, but this girl is a sadistic nymphomaniac," the actor said.
He asked, "What's that?"
Since it is who she is and I won't play her that way, you had better find out. Of course, I played her; there was nothing I could do to stop it. Hunt Stromberg, however, was not an idiot; he had only not been reading Freud. After doing some investigation, the character's greatest excesses were ultimately toned down. She wasn't Rebecca of Sunnybrook Farm, but from what I recall, she merely observed as others were spanked.

Put this on your lap, the director Charles Brabin instructed as I entered another scene. When I turned around, a python was being handed to me. "What?" I sighed and stared at this infinite thing that could easily suffocate me to death. I finally agreed to let them place the snake in my lap after much prodding. I gave it a touch, anticipating a chilly, slimy body. Instead, it was warmed up and heavily drugged so that it couldn't hurt me. Well, that poor critter broke my heart. On the scene, they all muttered, "Crazy woman," but after that, I paid close attention to my pet python.

Although Roddy McDowall persuaded me into watching it recently, I was surprised by how well Karloff and I did in that insane scene. Boris and I gave those comic-book characters some emotion and comedy, while everyone else just shrugged it off as something that didn't matter. Boris was a skilled performer who never made light of his frequently inferior material. When he says, "I want you to meet my ugly daughter," a beautiful creature wearing a jewel-encrusted Chinese costume designed by Adrian enters. In spite of these instances, I insisted that Fah Lo See be my final exotic, and she ended up becoming. In reality, the following stage of my career would absolutely destroy that one. A person made the suggestion to cast me as the Chinese empress in Fifty-five Days in Peking thirty years later. The response was an incredulous "Myrna Loy?" She is not capable of playing Chinese.

David O. Selznick was in charge of producing The Animal Kingdom at RKO, and Ned Griffith wanted to use me. During Rebound, Ned and I had developed a friendship. He knew what I was capable of as an actress, and I had a lot of respect for him as a filmmaker. Selznick disagreed and challenged him on my casting. David later claimed that he "leaped at the idea," even though anyone who knew me would have thought those Oriental siren roles were absurd. But in reality, he preferred Karen Morley to play the wife. Ned objected, saying that in Philip Barry's play the wife is more of a mistress and vice versa. "No, she isn't sexy enough," Ned said. After being let go from the Broadway production, Katharine Hepburn asserts that although she was interested in the role, "Myrna Loy got it because she was beautiful." David actually refused to allow me to test until Ned pulled a prank on him by convincing Leslie Howard to conduct a test with me late at night when no one was around.

I rested and watched the spectacle from my bed all day. Before I departed for the studio, my amazing Mexican maid Carolla, who always treated me like a queen, made scrambled eggs with garlic sausage. The sequence went down without a hitch, but Leslie Howard came off as restrained and uncharacteristically distant. I questioned Ned, "What did Mr. Howard think of me?"
Ned responded, "He thought you were very good, but questioned if you always eat so much garlic."

Leslie was a very picky vegetarian who was also a meticulous Englishman, as I subsequently discovered. He felt very sick from the scent of those Mexican sausages, but of course, he endured it like the gentleman he was. Oh, the experience of working with Leslie was wonderful. What a powerful, amazing actor he was, and yet how effortlessly he managed to pull it off. He always took the time to support me and ease me into a role that would take me further away from exotica. After seeing that photo, we came to like one another a lot. It could have turned into a true scrambola, if I had let it. Leslie's mild-mannered TV appearance belied his extreme impatience. That calm, svelte demeanor concealed a passionate temperament that showed on the scene. He attacked my home and begged me to flee with him to the South Seas after I rejected the temptation. He was compelled to drop everything and leave. Don't think he wasn't convincing either. He was married, though, and I wasn't into that kind of stuff. In addition, Arthur, who just so happened to be in New York on business, arrived back just in time. I did, however, adore Leslie.

I just heard a voice calling, "Myrna! Myrna!" while in London. Ruth Howard, Leslie's widow, was there. As we conversed, she inquired, "Have you seen Ronnie?" He is exactly like Leslie. That is their actor-turned-son, who resembles both of his parents. That day, Ruth said something extremely kind to Myrna that I will never forget: "Myrna, Leslie loved you so much." Oh, brother, little does she know, I thought.

I ultimately moved out of my mother's house around the time of The Animal Kingdom. When she saw Arthur and I were serious, she started to approach us. She didn't want me to get married because she wanted to stay in charge. She was living comfortably thanks to my labor, but she understood that would always be the case. She simply wasn't willing to let go. She needed to be a mother, but I was 27 and in a relationship. I simply packed a bag and left one evening; I sent Lou MacFarlane back for the rest of my belongings. Mother was so enraged that she spent a year in Europe.

Near Arthur, in Beverly Hills, I rented an apartment. After returning momentarily to the stage, Juliette took their son to her Warrenton, Virginia, family home. Even though she was certainly over Arthur, the two of them were still married. Although Juliette showed no signs of antagonism when he took me to see her in Dodsworth, he said that she wouldn't grant him a divorce. That evening, Arthur's complete lack of emotion was the issue. In addition to casually bringing his female companion backstage to meet his estranged wife, he also had no problem standing by in the wings while a harsh stage director coached her after the performance. He ignored the possibility that our presence there would make her feel embarrassed, which I saw and quickly discounted as an example of his insensitivity. Such senses are diminished when one is in love.

Although we spent four years courting or living together, we were able to keep our relationship out of the public eye, which would have given the columnists a field day. Everyone participated, but no one discussed it. Only the obvious ones—those who didn't hide—were made public; not the subdued ones. In actuality, I can only think of one joke about us during that period, which was in the Hollywood Reporter and mentioned Leslie Howard "carrying a torch for Arthur Hornblow's paramour."

You understand, back then, everything had to be flawless both on and off the screen, including all relationships to be in order, all hair to be in its appropriate place, and no creases in your outfits or personal affairs. The consummate perfectionist David Selznick consistently pursued an improbable ideal. He constantly told me to get my ears repaired because he thought they protruded too far. He would have the makeup artist apply them close to my head if I had my hair up or swept back in a scene. My ears began to pop loose as the lights grew hotter. "Cut!" the director would command. Who is the makeup artist? Then we would start afresh. I was worn out and frustrated by it. It irked me.

Despite my objections, David made arrangements to keep me at RKO so that I could work with John Barrymore again—this time as his leading lady—on the film Topaze. I ran into Jack as I was heading to see the director, Harry D'Arrast, and he went right by me without saying a word. Remembering our arguments about Don Juan, I thought, "Oh, God, he doesn't want me. But that was six years ago—how could he possibly still hold that against me? When I went to Harry, he advised me to ignore him.

Someone rapped on the door of my dressing room the following morning. "Myrna, Harry tells me that I slighted you yesterday," said Mr. Barrymore himself. Well, I was a little perplexed. I couldn't decide which of the three of you to bow to when I saw you.

That he had been drinking hadn't occurred to me, but what a classy way to make up for a mistake. I was thinking about Don Juan and expected him to blow out at some point, but after the first day, there were no issues. He frequently made jokes about his drinking, but he stayed sober on the set and took the film extremely seriously. To me, Topaze was very important to him. He wasn't the same rogue I remembered at Warners; instead, he was generous, supportive, and depressed during our sequences. At this point, he had started keeping exotic fish in tanks. He developed interests in a variety of things, including, as I recall, rearing hens at one point. He had built a pond in what he dubbed his "Chinese tenement" on Tower Road since fishing had become his new hobby. He mentioned buying rare tropical fish when I inquired about Dolores and their two children, so I imagined things were unstable at home. But on the set, he was a lamb, utterly adorable. I don't know if he was just out of gas, but I consider myself lucky to have been a part of one of his best movies.

Irving Thalberg sent for me to come back to M-G-M. Thalberg is frequently referred to as the master producer, but I haven't seen any proof of it. I had no idea at the time that he had brought me to Metro or had any special feelings for me. He kept me waiting in his outside office for a very long time. He turned away from me, glanced out the window, and began talking as soon as I entered the vehicle. My back rose, I guess. Bad manners irritate me a lot. You're aware that was Miss Loy. He swiveled his chair back toward me as I turned to go. I replied quite pompously, "Thank you. "I was raised to look people in the eye when I speak to them."

He responded, shocked but unperturbed, "What?" He was a handsome man with a terrific face and deep, penetrating eyes, albeit he was always a little bit unwell and had shoulders that leaned forward somewhat. Despite my reaction, he said, "Myrna, you're awfully bashful. There is no justification for you to be. By establishing a barrier between you and the audience, it harms you. You need to break past the curtain and seize the attention of the crowd. Give it your all. They accept it, and they like you. They think the world of you. Make it work for you because you are both attractive enough for the movies and making good progress here, both of things I had previously questioned.

I mean, I knew I was shy, but I hadn't understood how much it affected my job. The fact that Thalberg discovered it is intriguing. He had no idea who I was; well, we had met at events and the such, but we had never actually spent time together. However, he noticed this, and oddly enough, it was at that point that I finally made the decision to leave home and start a new life for myself, lifting the curtain in more ways than one. I originally had the impression that M-G-M had intentions for me after that encounter with Irving Thalberg.

According to Minna Wallis, they were pushing her incredibly hard as they started to grow her at Metro. I requested a raise from Louis B. Mayer. I will always remember that day. Outside of the studio, Mayer and I were close friends, but as soon as I entered, he asked, "Now what do you want?" I proclaimed, "I want a raise for Myrna Loy." "She's getting so much," he exclaimed. "so much. so much. so much." I remarked, "That's not enough." Then, and I'll never forget it, he started crying. What are you doing to me? he kept wailing as tears streamed from his eyes. You're attempting to destroy me. It didn't surprise me because I was aware of those brief outbursts he had. I finally received Myrna's rise after putting up with some of his faking to cry and moving on.

In the 1920s, every woman's idea of heaven was to be whisked away to an oasis by Valentino, Ramon Novarro, or any respectable imitation. In The Barbarian, that's exactly what happened to me. Ramon, an Egyptian dragoman, falls for my charms, breaks my window with orchids, and kidnaps me. Unfortunately, movie fans' tastes were evolving in 1933. Even though Ramon was still a major celebrity and Metro's reigning exotic lover, things were starting to go wrong for him. He was aware that his career was in jeopardy. That wasn't an issue because he had prudently invested his earnings, but it's still very upsetting to see someone's career irrevocably go apart.

Ramon was actually a quiet, kind man, much like many of those so-called great lovers. In that movie, we grew close, but the studio abused that friendship. The sensitive information about our "torrid romance," which was obviously common knowledge to everyone but the participants, was revealed to me when I picked up a newspaper. It was ridiculous. The publicity team had picked a really unusual match because Ramon wasn't even interested in the women and I was only seeing Arthur. I had never experienced that specific circumstance before. I raised hell because it enraged me. I'm not sure if that had anything to do with it, but it never occurred again.

The Barbarian, on the other hand, was a wild, wacky film with settings in the vast sand dunes outside Yuma, Arizona. I took my first ever camel ride. She had a bad habit of biting and spitting everywhere, so to this day I can still recall her name, Rosie. On the sound stage, I encountered yet another danger: a vintage Hollywood bathing scene. They spread rose petals over the water when I was securely immersed in a sunken marble bathtub, positioning guys to stir the petals with long, toothed rakes. They appeared to be overly enthusiastic as they kept shoving those rose petals closer and closer to cover me. A ring of recognizable faces—friends and neighbors from Culver City who worked in the studio—greeted me as I gazed up. They were working hard to defend the virtue of a local girl while they were unaware that I was wearing clothing that had a flesh tone. Although it was quite nice, it didn't work. I was made to look completely naked in the shot that some magazine photographer took inside and then syndicated over the world.

Ramon and I once saw a ruckus up ahead while being taken from one set to another. People were running erratically and staring up into the sky. Our director, Sam Wood, hurried over to us and exclaimed, "There was an earthquake just now!" Although Ramon and I were in the moving automobile and didn't experience the initial shock, the aftershocks were so powerful that they decided to cancel the rest of the day's work. On that day, M-G-M was filled with people running furiously in all directions, resembling the Mack Sennett lot. Robert Montgomery became disoriented in the baffles—those sort of winged panels—when the lights in the sound booth went out and he rushed about like a whirling dervish in an attempt to get away. Louis B. Mayer and his horrified coworkers fled for the outside stairwell going from his second-floor office when the ancient executive building began to shake. Because of Mayer's size, the ordinarily subservient lieutenants started pushing and shoving each other until they all were caught on the shaky wooden stairs.

When George Bernard Shaw traveled to California in 1933, he lodged with William Randolph Hearst and his mistress, Marion Davies, at the Hearst property in San Simeon. That greatly pleased me because the dramatist had been criticized for his Socialism and liberal ideologies for years in Hearst's newspapers. Since I was familiar with his life and politics and had seen or read most of his plays, this relationship struck me as being really odd. Despite the fact that Marion had a major crush on me, I never visited San Simeon. We used to like talking and laughing at events together since she had a kind heart. But Hearst's politics and mine just didn't mesh. Shaw, it seems, operated under the principle of noblesse oblige.

Shaw's official tour guide in Hollywood was still Marion. She continued to work for M-G-M, so Mayer had the opportunity to host one of his inescapable celebrity lunches. On the When Ladies Meet set, it was mentioned that Shaw will drop by after lunch. Bob Montgomery actually leapt up and down because he was so excited. He was so distraught by the notion of meeting the great guy, in fact. The possibility also excited me, although not to the point of excitement. Bob suggested, "Let's go up to makeup and acquire a lot of long white beards like his. "We'll all wear them and surprise him," she said. I reacted by saying, "Noooo, we don't do that. We don't do that." That was how lost Bob was.

Bob, Ann Harding, and I were doing a scenario when who should enter the room? After formal introductions, he approached me and questioned whether one of my lines was necessary. This wasn't helpful, and I assumed he was just trying to make me feel uncomfortable. "Well, Mr. Shaw," I said, "that's the line, and that's how the director wants it. That is how things work. In other words, I made a weak case to him. He simply gave me a good look and assessed my stature, which should have been threatening given his piercing blue eyes and satyr's sneer. Miss Loy, however, was having none of it as usual. I wasn't readily won over by any of these outstanding people because I was raised by self-respecting folks. Of course, I wished we had talked more, but it turned out Shaw was a devil, a very mischievous man who found fun in teasing other people.

He must have done these things on purpose because after trying to provoke me and failing, he attempted Ann Harding. Ann noted that she had performed in Captain Brassbound's Conversion at the Pennsylvania Hedgerow Theatre in a polite and respectful manner. He roared, "Did you, now?" It was most likely a pirate performance. He berated her, threatened legal action, and completely destroyed her confidence before acting very horribly and leaving the scene.

Ann sprinted to her changing room and sobbed. Curiously, it was through that terrible event that I had my one and only chance to meet Ann Harding. Although we had both completed The Animal Kingdom, we had not collaborated. She remained a very private person, a superb actress entirely lacking star attitude, but withdrawn, despite the fact that When Ladies Meet provided us multiple scenes together as the title implies.

A completely different situation involved Alice Brady. Her own theater and silent-film careers had been impressive, and her father, William Brady, was a well-known theatrical producer, but this hadn't made her turn away. She was wonderful, humorous, and endearing. She believed it was appropriate for her pets—dogs, cats, and various other creatures—to be named after characters from the Greek original after appearing in O'Neill's Mourning Becomes Electra. The canine Agamemnons, feline Clytemnestras, and twittering Electras who overran Alice's home were characteristic of her spontaneous irreverence. She was adored by Bob Montgomery, and since they both had sharp minds, they were hilarious company. We formed a little group of three and periodically visited her home or went out to eat after work. Pictures rarely capture that kind of casual friendliness; since things move so quickly, it's difficult to get to know individuals.

The fact that W.S. Van Dyke directed Penthouse was a major selling point. One of the most significant things to happen to me ever turned out to be that. He shouted down the commissary, "This girl's going to be a big star!" "She'll be a star next year." Van Dyke actually came up with the first part, which was written especially for me. Oh, some of them do that, you know, ramble on and on about this, that, and the other. It was originally titled The Sailor and the Lady for Clark Gable and me, but Max Baer, a real prizefighter, and I ultimately changed the title to The Prizefighter and the Lady. The narrative by Frances Marion was better than the title suggests, and Woody Van Dyke, as usual, improved it.

Woody is the fastest director I've ever worked with, but he still managed to give each project a unique touch. He was known for his spontaneity both on and off the set. He was full of practical pranks, including wiring chairs so that when you sat down, you would receive a terrible shock, and he gloated whenever Max Baer's fear of mice was brought up. Nothing but placing a mouse on Max's chair as soon as he sat down would do. So, after taking one glimpse at that small mouse, this magnificent man screamed and flew away like a bat out of hell. Despite his lack of acting expertise, he still maintained his presence on screen and delivered a strong performance. Additionally, he appeared in the part. I adored how he would lean towards the ropes before throwing himself back, his gorgeous physique absolutely shining. Baer and Primo Carnera squared off in the main event, with Jack Dempsey serving as the referee. They traveled from all around to watch us shoot the fight because Baer was the exceptional challenger and Carnera was the legitimate heavyweight champion.

Primo Camera was a remarkable monster with massive hands and feet, standing at about seven feet tall. There was still room for the crew to sign after the entire cast signed one of his sneakers for him.

He appeared to be a depressed man because, in a sense, he was a freak of nature and this bothered him. The next year, he was defeated by Max for the heavyweight title. Ironically, Max had been emulating Carnera's fighting style while they were filming The Prizefighter and the Lady.

Night Flight, which stars the Barrymore brothers, Helen Hayes, Clark Gable, Bob Montgomery, and, for the first time, Myrna Loy, gets crammed in there somehow. It is also famous for having an all-star ensemble. We created that image in fragments, in the form of separate episodes featuring unrelated individuals. No one save Bill Gargan, whom I had adored since The Animal Kingdom, was present, not Jack, Helen, or anyone else. He embarks on a fatal trip in our really good scene, as does everyone else in that photo, it seemed.

Clark Gable and I weren't coworkers on Night Flight, but Minna Wallis made the introduction at that time. Every year, the so-called Hollywood elite had the Mayfair Ball; everyone who was anyone would dress to the nines, head over to the Ambassador, and get down and dirty. "I'm taking Mr. and Mrs. Gable," Minna announced. "I figured you might want to meet Clark," I said. He had become the talk of Hollywood at that point and was considered hot by all the ladies, including my buddy Lou MacFarlane. He was rumored to be constantly on the go, arriving at the studio after everyone else and snapping garters left and right. But at the dance, he behaved like the ideal gentleman: attentive but not domineering. We danced that night to "Dancing in the Dark," and he was lively and friendly, a fantastic dancer, so every time I hear that song, I think of him. .. It was divine. When we returned home, we first dropped off Minna, leaving the Gables and I in the back seat of the limo. Rhea, Clark's second wife, was much older than him and had a matronly demeanor despite being charming the entire evening. I noticed Clark was starting to get a little smitten while we were driving to my mother's place. While his wife was seated right there next to him, he began to edge closer to me. Of course, by then he was undoubtedly loaded. To some degree, we all were.

I was led to the door by Clark. I turned to open it when he knelt down and gave me a "monkey bite." (It left a days-long scar on my neck.) He took two or three steps off the porch and into the hedge after I turned around and shoved him. I recall that when he stumbled back, he grinned a little, which only enraged me more. It was merely the thought of his wife waiting in the car. I had a lot of boyfriends before, but this was different since it wasn't right. I didn't want to take part.

When I barged inside the house, what did I discover? Lou MacFarlane was stooping to see out the window. In an effort to get a glimpse of her hero, she stayed the night. I blustered, "That rude, ignorant person," asking, "What could you possibly see in that person?"
She remained composed and added, "Myrna, I wouldn't care if he couldn't read."

Soon after that, I ran into Clark at the studio, and he was walking straight by me with his nose in the air. We were cast together for Men in White the next thing I knew. I'm in serious trouble; wow, this is going to be something. Elizabeth Allan, a stunning English girl in the cast, and Clark had a rather serious relationship when the movie first began. Clark would greet Elizabeth Allan with coffee and pastries every morning. Clark would pack up and, just to get on my nerves, stroll right past me to Elizabeth since the crew usually set out sweet breads. He was making me pay. It was difficult for us to appear to be in love on camera while he practically ignored me. But we managed to do it. That Dutchman simply wouldn't accept no as an option.

I had made fifteen photographs in less than two years at Metro. They exhausted us completely. Without rehearsing, you would move from one scene to the next without always knowing what your part would be. Your afternoon lines in the commissary would be handed to you, so you could learn them during lunch. Those alleged moguls horribly mistreated us. Actually, we weren't much more than mere chattels, but it was still a worthwhile experience. You learned acting on the job; you didn't need acting school. If they were going to build you, they created you to last.

The Great Depression was still going strong. I was grateful to have a job and apprehensive about not seizing every chance. I therefore barely existed outside of the set. After a long day of work, I was simply too exhausted to think about anything but sleeping, which naturally put pressure on my already tense relationship with Arthur Hornblow. I finally had enough and called the studio's talent coordinator, Benny Thau, who was always helpful: "Benny, send me my week's salary." I'm spending every penny I have by traveling to Honolulu. I boarded the Monterey with Shirley Hughes, my stand-in, and we sailed for Hawaii, where Betty and Bob Black were stationed. Bob was the only enlisted guy selected out of ten thousand applicants and had just received his appointment as a second lieutenant in the Medical Corps.

Betty Black joked that Myrna used to check in occasionally to see how the marriage she started was going. Even though the Thin Man movies hadn't yet begun, she was already well-known, so when her boat landed, she was greeted with a royal welcome and had leis piled up above her head. She initially remained at the Royal Hawaiian, but when guests wouldn't leave her alone, she joined us at Schofield Barracks so she could rest. She was followed there as well. Because of her name and the roles she performed, Chun Hoon, one of the wealthiest men on the island, believed Myrna was of Chinese descent. He hosted this expensive party for her at his magnificent estate, which had a large lanai. There were Hawaiian and Chinese orchestras playing, and the meal had 35 dishes, starting with bird's-nest soup and continuing throughout. Chun Hoon would lift his glass and offer a toast to the following course after each course. Despite the small glasses, the beverages were potent. We nearly failed to finish the meal. All of the highest representatives from the embassies and islands were present, along with the Chinese consul, to meet Myrna. Remember, we were in pre-annexation ancient Hawaii. This was a rare instance of a highly important Chinese patriarch opening his doors to Hawaii's international society.

Myrna was the center of attention, and everything seemed to be happening in a dream to her—everything was great, etc.—but her thoughts were still on Arthur. Everything else is a side matter when Myrna is in love. She had departed despite the fact that his marriage was undoubtedly over because he had decided against filing for divorce. You see, Myrna wanted to be a man's wife and wanted to marry him if she loved him. She has never been one to have extramarital affairs because she has always aspired to be the ideal wife that she would later play in movies.

People were bothering her, so we left the post. We were never given any privacy. When I opened the door, a woman would ram her young child inside. If tiny so-and-so wanted to touch Miss Loy's hand, could she? She had met the prominent Scottish plantation owners, the Beckleys, who had intermarried with the Hawaiian royal family, on the voyage there. Princess Liliuokalani, a relative of Mrs. Beckley, had a relationship with John Gilbert during the time. They were so captivated by Myrna that they gave her the use of their private estate on the opposite side of the island from Honolulu. We ate fresh fruit and swam while living the authentic Hawaiian way of life. Myrna wanted a tranquil vacation, but throughout the whole time she worried because Arthur hadn't called. A wire stating that Arthur wanted Myrna to return so they could make plans to get married was waiting when Bob returned to Schofield. After leaving Arthur, she returned to her job.

We just got back from a wonderful vacation on the Mariposa with Shirley. Because John Gilbert was on board, that trip, which took place in February 1934, ended with a very sorrowful return. He was one of the most famous actors in silent films and the biggest victim of sound. On occasion, a slender, ghostly man would show up on an upper deck somewhere, accompanied by a male nurse who was watching nervously. After his Metro contract was terminated and his brief marriages to Ina Claire and Virginia Bruce, he appeared to be so far gone—nursing his wounds, I assume. Princess Liliuokalani had rejected him after he had traveled to Hawaii in search of her. He was making an effort to put his jumbled life back together, but it remained jumbled. Never would it be. Over the next two years, he slowly drank himself to death.

They immediately assigned me a job in Manhattan Melodrama, which led to the death of John Dillinger, Public Enemy No. 1. After he had seen the movie, FBI officers shot him dead outside of the

Chicago Biograph Theatre. He claimed to be a fan of Myrna Loy and came out to see me. I think the concept of the artwork, not my fatal attractions, drew him, but even so, I've always felt a bit bad about it. Poor soul, they filled him to the brim with holes.

A mafia story, but an intriguing one that would be regularly replayed again and again, was Manhattan Melodrama. In the streets of New York, two friends grow up. One becomes a gangster named Clark Gable, while the other takes on the role of William Powell, a governor who must authorize the killing of a buddy. Beginning as Gable's girl, I eventually became the governor's bride. Strangely enough, I don't remember much about my interactions with Clark at that point, but I remember that he appeared okay toward me at the time—not overly enthusiastic, but there wasn't time. I was racing from pillar to post while Woody Van Dyke was the director. That picture truly doesn't start until Bill enters the room.

Before we even met, I acted in my first scene with Bill, a nighttime scenario that was filmed on the back lot. It seems like Woody was too busy to make an introduction. I was told to exit a building, through a crowd, and get into an unknown car. I flung open the car door as Woody yelled "Action," leaped inside, and landed directly on William Powell's lap. Miss Loy, I assume," he said, casually turning to face her. "Mr. Powell?" I exclaimed. I met the man who would become my co-star in fourteen movies in this way.

You can notice an interesting change in how I play my connections with Clark and Bill in that picture. My women were naturally matched to the men's personalities by me. In those days, male-female relationships were considerably more clearly defined. In accordance with the script, the mores, and the men's skills, it was my responsibility to bring life to those connections. Love scenes were challenging for Clark, for example, who suffered greatly from the macho issue. Being sensitive might have undermined his image of a manly man, therefore he kept a very stiff upper lip. Because Carole Lombard had a harsh quality and he liked girls with that quality, I always played it a little rough with him, giving him what-for to bring him out. Of course, at first I was unaware of everything. I had an intuitive reaction to it.

In my game with Bill, I was different. I kept a distance from him and was occasionally shocked because of his innate sense of humor and outrageousness. We had a strange connection from the very first scene onwards—a sense of rhythm, total understanding, and an intuition for how each of us could bring out the best in the other. You can see this odd—I don't know what to call it—relationship in all of our collaborative work. It was not thinking. The same thing would be audible if you heard us conversing in a room. He would gently tease me, and a sort of mixture would come out that appeared to please folks. Whatever the source, it was magical and Woody Van Dyke brought it to life in our following photograph, which is possibly the one most associated with my one hundred and twenty-four characteristics.

Woody responded with a script based on Dashiell Hammett's top-selling book The Thin Man, which Alexander Woollcott hailed as "the best detective story yet written in America." For the first time since Love Me Tonight, it promised a humorous role, which I adored. My jobs had been very straightforward up to that point, though I had occasionally cracked a joke. But a problem had arisen by the time I told Woody about it. I was rejected for the role by Mayer. Powell is capable of playing a detective; he has already portrayed Philo Vance. Yes, that's OK, but Myrna needs to be excluded. For casting me, there was no precedent. Oh, they were in a nasty fight! Woody remained adamant, "She's OK. I shoved her into my pool. He had put me to the test, and it seemed I passed. Mayer bowed down when Woody hinted about leaving, but only under certain restrictions. If The Thin Man wasn't ready by the time I began Stamboul Quest in three weeks, Woody could have me. It took two months—at least six weeks—to bring in a picture like that, so perhaps he thought Woody would back down. They got their just desserts from Woody. With two days for retakes, he completed The Thin Man in sixteen days.

He was referred to as "One-take Van Dyke." He wouldn't even attempt a cover shot if he could successfully complete the task the first time. If actors perform a scenario again, they will inevitably lose interest in it, he claimed. "That fire is what gives the picture on the screen life." Speed allowed him to achieve his desired spontaneity. Naturally, he had us riled up, but by that point, I could enter, look at fresh lines, and do them. Because the scripts were always changing back then, you had to. You could study the day before a lot of the time, but not always. You had to have the discipline to comply with Woody's demands for remarkable actions otherwise you couldn't work with him. Eventually, he grew too quick; it turned into an obsession. The Thin Man was made, however, by his pace and spontaneity.

Even if it was the Ritz bar, what other director would introduce his star with a flawless three-point landing on the floor of the room? I was expected to enter the room while wearing a stylish outfit, carrying numerous parcels, and leashing Asta. You may fall. asked Woody. "Can you perform a fall?" "I've never worked for Mack Sennett, but I'm a dancer," I remarked. I think I can pull it off. I was completely committed to Woody and would have done anything for him. He explained, "You just trip yourself, and then go right down."

Without any practice, we shot it after he placed a camera on the ground and marked the spot where he wanted me to land. I had to be insane. I had the opportunity to commit suicide, but my dancing training paid off. I rushed in with Asta and all of those parcels, stumbled over myself, fell to the floor, slid across it, and struck the target with my chin. It was amazing beyond belief!

Because we enjoyed what we were doing, the filming process went really smoothly. The only issue arose when Nick Charles revealed the identity of the cockrobin's killer. While I only occasionally gave him those sage Nora Charles looks, poor Bill groused loudly about having to memorize so many lines. Waiters brought out oysters on the half shell as everyone settled down to a large dinner table, and Bill started to figure out the mystery. He made a heroic effort before mumbling, "I don't know what I'm talking about." However, Woody didn't mind as long as it continued to move. So we would start over, and those oysters would come back. They refused to send fresh ones, and as the shooting continued under the lights, they started to putrefy. Nobody wanted to see another oyster after we wrapped up that scene.

Our producer, Hunt Stromberg, didn't receive a ton of funding for The Thin Man. By no means was it regarded as a major motion picture; a three-week shooting period typically indicated a B feature. We didn't anticipate the outcome that occurred. Absolutely none. Although we already knew we enjoyed it and found it to be entertaining, the response was completely unexpected. The brass at M-G-M were shocked.

According to Samuel Marx, who was in charge of M-G-M's story department at the time, we went to the first preview with dread and trembling. The businessmen, including Hunt Stromberg—who was already uneasy—went down to Huntington Park. We didn't know whether this type of humor would work when I paid $14,000 for this brisk detective thriller. They were having fun with murder, and they were a married pair who acted with complete sophistication, both of which were two novel characteristics that terrified the living daylights out of the entire studio. "Gus, how many has he had?" Myrna asks Bill as she joins him at the bar. When the bartender calls out "Seven," she adds, "Set 'em up," and matches her husband's drink for drink. That might have given post-Prohibition audiences who were still wary of social drinking a shock.

Even Powell and Loy's marriage posed a danger because back then, weddings took place towards the conclusion of the film rather at the beginning. Marriage wasn't meant to be enjoyable. According to Myrna, "I think it's a dirty trick to bring me all the way to New York just to make me a widow of me." Bill says, "You wouldn't be a widow for very long." She nods in agreement, "You bet I wouldn't!" And in response, he says, "Not with all your money." These are wonderful lines, but nobody knew how people would react to them the night of the preview.

I can only tell you that following that preview, it was a night of great celebration on the Huntington Park promenade. The entire event broke with convention in a number of ways, but it appeared to be a success. That initial preview served as a thermometer that displayed the level of heat this team was producing. The characteristics of Nick and Nora Charles as well as Myrna Loy and William Powell all contributed to their chemistry. You had to keep putting them together; it was automatic. The response was so strong that it never subsided.

The Thin Man eventually made me after eighty or so pictures—a startling fact that Lawrence J. Quirk's Films of Myrna Loy recently came to mind. I was now on par with the general public and the studio. It stimulated the media. Since then, they have referred to me as "the perfect wife," which has typed me in a similar way to how those vamp roles had. But, perfect or not, this wife thing at least resembled my personality more. In the sense of being the virginal, pure creature who seemed to be so greatly admired, Nora was far from the ideal wife. I didn't act that way on-screen or off. Men would marry such women to be the mothers of their children, but they were typically abandoned by the men sooner or later.

I like Gore Vidal's description of me as "the eternal good-sex woman-wife," which does not imply perfection in a puritanical sense. Who among men would desire a flawless wife? We didn't try to disguise the reality that sex is a necessary component of marriage, which is what made the Thin Man series entertaining and successful. But it was clever and executed with grace and charm. The Charleses also had a very high level of tolerance for one another's flaws. It wasn't any cloying utopian perfection—quite the opposite—that made their marriage entertaining to observe. Oh my gosh! The Thin Man practically invented contemporary marriage on film. In the past, people got married and had happy ever afters, but the undercurrents were never visible.

Nobody ever fails to inquire about Bill or Asta in a day of my existence. Recently, the delivery person for my afternoon newspaper gave me back my money with the notation, "Never a charge for Nora Charles." That's immortality right there! Over the years, a number of wire-haired terriers played the role of our scene-stealing pet, but we were not permitted to become close with any of them. Their trainer was concerned that it would cause the dogs to lose focus. Skippy, the first one, bit me once, so our relationship wasn't quite ideal. My connection to Bill was. Contrary to popular misconception, we were never actually married or even close to being so, but we did become extremely good friends. Oh sure, there were moments when Bill had feelings for me and vice versa, but we never pursued them. We found a solution and remained friends. Nobody in today's culture seems to grasp how you may be extremely close to and deeply in love with someone without having sexual relations with him. Bill and I would have argued if we had been lovers. And it would have been worse if we had been married.

William Powell revealed, "Even my dearest friends never cease to remind me that the smartest thing I ever did was to marry Myrna Loy on the screen. And, I might say, it was the most delightful. I never saw Myrna have a temper tantrum, scream and rave, or storm off the set while we were married in thirteen films, including Libeled Lady (I suppose we were married; it was a little confusing). Even in the most trying circumstances, she never lets her emotions get too close to the surface and maintains her composure. On set, she would occasionally want to sit by herself while other times she would feel rowdy and want to pull pranks.

We forgot about technique, camera angles, and mics while we worked on a scene together. We weren't performing. We were only two people operating in perfect unison. I frequently performed with an actress who appeared to be positioned behind a plate-glass window from me; there was no eye contact at all. But Myrna has the fortunate ability to listen while the other actor delivers his lines, unlike some women who only care about themselves. She possesses the acting chemistry needed to bring out the best in characters.

Without her, The Thin Man would not have been the hit that it was. She transformed into every man's ideal of what a wife should be when the bed rolled beneath her in the hangover scene and she looked up at me with the ice bag on her head and said, "You pushed me." She was stunning and glamorous with a sense of humor, provocative and feminine without being sweet or sharp, and the ideal woman who never lost her temper, jumped to conclusions, or nagged a guy. Men-Must-Marry-Myrna Clubs started to form. Hearty Nigel Bruce finally gave in and sent her his first letter of admiration. Jimmy Stewart made the declaration, "I shall only marry Myrna Loy," as women sobbed.

In Stamboul Quest, I made my final stand in exotica as Fräulein Doktor, the spy who apprehended Mata Hari. I played the Fräulein while she was still alive. Fear of libel kept the script vague the entire time since she had developed a drug addiction, gone insane, and ended up in a Swiss sanatorium. It's a complex spy tale that seems somewhat hazy to me today, except that I wore a gorgeous black picture hat and loved George Brent at the time. Although he wasn't unpleasant to me, he was a good actor who occasionally asserted his independence, especially when the script was constantly changing. He produced a great deal of work but was never a true superstar.

To take advantage of The Thin Man's popularity, they hurriedly ushered me into Evelyn Prentice along with Bill Powell. Pure melodrama is rendered a little bit more tolerable by William K. Howard's direction—my old champion at Fox—in which I play the wife of a well-known trial lawyer who believes she has murdered someone. Going into this thing was a little tedious since The Thin Man had been so great for us and such a blast to do. Bill experienced sporadic depression as a result. I had never seen him in that light. "People don't know it, but I'm primarily Irish," he said. "We experience these dark times."

Apart from Roz, who made her film debut in that picture, I don't remember much else about it. Rozlind Russell. She had a pretty little role back then, so I didn't get to see her much, but because of her beautiful extroverted attitude, she was hard to miss. Because of a note John Considine sent me on the green interoffice paper that Metro officials used, I can't help but think of the film's producer. I don't know why I've kept it all these years, but I have. Possibly as a caution:

Dear Myrna:
Mr. and Mrs. Erich Von Stroheim are in dire need and several of their old friends on the lot have suggested that we make up a Christmas Fund to at least help them out of their immediate difficulties.

If you feel inclined to join in this much needed collection, will you please give John Farrow your check for $25.00 or more and make the same payable to Reverend John O'Donnell, who has done more than anyone else to help the Von Stroheims through their very serious troubles. Father O'Donnell will give Von a list of our names, together with the check, as I am sure that Von would be much happier about the matter if he knew the names of those who thought of him at this time.
John

Columbia borrowed me from Metro for Frank Capra's Broadway Bill. Because I would increase my box office, my home studio would be able to sell or lend me for much more than my weekly wage. In most cases, if you didn't enjoy the part, they wouldn't send you. It Happened One Night was Frank's prior film, for which he attempted to borrow me. It was rejected by me, and Louis B. Mayer supported my decision. Frank claims that despite Harry Cohn's persistent pleading, Mayer said, "Harry, I never ask one of my little girls to play a part she doesn't want." Oh, I've received criticism for rejecting the photo. For many years, Frank gave it to me. I still hear Lou MacFarlane, who pleaded with me to do it, saying, "I told you so!" But let me just say right now that they sent me the worst script I've ever read—completely unrelated to the one they actually shot. I've had other people confirm that. Nobody believes me, even though Bob Montgomery declined the male lead for the same reason. That girl was playable only in its original form. She's escaping because being wealthy bores her in the midst of the Great Depression, after all. Naturally, the script came to me during one of those times when I had become numb from nonstop picture-making.

Broadway Bill was a unique situation. Making that script was enjoyable because it immediately captured my attention. I recently viewed it and wondered, "Oh my gods, could I ever have been that young?" Van Dyke worked faster than Frank Capra, who took his time. He occasionally allowed us to continue with our own ideas before ending a session. Despite the fact that none of our ideas were really sound, occasionally something valuable resulted from them. Frank, a graduate of Mack Sennett, enjoyed improvising business on the set. Not that I was very aware of his technique—being aware of such things is very harmful for an actress because it limits her performance. I just thought he was smart and trusted him.

I spent a lot of time listening to Frank's life narrative, which was an intriguing Horatio Alger tale about how he started out and ultimately became a director. He said absolutely nothing about my decision to reject It Happened One Night, which shocked me a little. Of course, it hadn't yet won the 1934 Academy Awards, and Claudette Colbert and Clark Gable were cast, which was a very good choice. They looked fantastic in the final product, as it turned out. Additionally, Claudette possessed the necessary legs.

Later, Frank had a lot of fun with me on the radio when he said, "She turned me down." So I assumed he could be a little bitter. He recently revealed that they entirely revised the script after I'd seen it, which pleased me. I've always felt a bit guilty about declining, but not too much, since if I hadn't, I might not have had the opportunity to perform in The Thin Man that year. Ironically, the Academy received a barrage of complaints the same year about Bette Davis's lack of nomination for Of Human Bondage and my for The Thin Man. Because of the outcry, voting regulations were really disregarded for the first and only time, allowing members to disregard printed ballots and write in any name. Naturally, by that point, the majority of the ballots had already been mailed in, making all of the winners—including Claudette—official nominees. Since then, Bette has won a few awards, but I've never even received a nomination. Oftentimes, comedians do not receive it.

Then, were Arthur and I wed? No, we still weren't married; we were just long-term partners. Even when I became pregnant, he continued to claim that he was unable to obtain a divorce. Years later, his first wife informed me that this wasn't the case and that he hadn't been making an effort. I'm not sure. He eventually had to pay a sizable divorce settlement, so perhaps he wanted to postpone doing so. Maybe he was afraid of getting remarried. I agreed to an abortion because I wanted to prevent being pregnant again and because I knew he loved me and that he loved him. I regret it, yet in a way it was a blessing. Being a wife in this industry is challenging enough without having to also be a mother. The kids don't get treated fairly.

I'm aware that some individuals, like Joan Bennett, handled it admirably, but that's how I felt about it. Surrogate children, including my godchildren, my stepson Terry and his family, and the kids of friends and relatives with whom I've always been able to identify, have allayed any regrets and any underlying sense of sacrifice.

Arthur possessed talent. His attention to detail and sense of perfection—which eventually turned into an obsession—were key factors in his success as a producer. He continued to produce excellent movies after leaving Goldwyn in 1933, first for Paramount, then for M-G-M, and eventually on his own, with titles like Easy Living, Hold Back the Dawn, The Major and the Minor, Gaslight, The Asphalt Jungle, Oklahoma!, and Witness for the Prosecution. He introduced me to a different facet of the motion picture industry because I wasn't aware of the entire scope of a producer's role. He invited me to see previews with him while I observed him assess crowd response—something I rarely did with my own films. At Metro, actors weren't urged to attend previews.

We went to Huntington Park to see a preview of the movie Mississippi, which was directed by Eddie Sutherland and stars W. C. Fields. Fields appeared to be just how he appeared in the movies; he was this roistering guy who was funny all the time and extremely funny. He didn't seem to notice me at dinner after that, as far as I can remember. I suppose he tolerated me. His mother or another woman must have mistreated him as a child because he didn't like women, as you may know. It was something incredibly odd. In Mississippi, one of his remarks was, "I'd sooner stick a knife in my mother's back." As opposed to that, he declared, "I'd sooner stick a fork in my mother's back." He wanted it that way, and Eddie was unable to convince him otherwise. The distinction between a knife and a fork in that situation just seems so horrifying.

At that critical period, exposure to Arthur's universe helped me develop socially as well. We all went out to dinner one night when he took Charles Laughton out for Ruggles of Red Gap. Charles and his wife Elsa Lanchester had the British-exclusive verbal dexterity and were intelligent and well-traveled. I doubt I spoke much at dinner because I was a little intimidated by them. Who should appear by the pool the following day in the Garden of Allah, where I briefly resided, but Mr. Laughton himself? He was wrapped in a large towel and appeared to be Emperor Nero. He sat down beside me and said, "Well, hullo," as if he were a long-lost buddy. You know what you remind me of, "Myrna"—he used my first name, which made me happy—"? The Venus of Milo sculpture is located near Hollywood and Vine.

Well, I enjoyed that because, in those early days of stardom, I was confused and unsure of myself as I entered a new field. Despite the fact that I was scarcely a Venus de Milo, such insightful smiles demonstrated Charles' perceptiveness. He noticed a side of myself that my expertise typically conceals. I wasn't reserved among my family or close friends, but a lot of successful individuals were entering my life, which could be scary. It wasn't a paralyzing kind of thing; if provoked, I could handle a Barrymore or a Shaw. But the majority of us in the industry often act cautiously. When we were working in Cape Cod, for instance, Hank Fonda remarked, "You know, I'm very shy." He was also a pretty bashful person. Sometimes it can be misread. You're viewed as a nasty snob by others. I wasn't at all, but in addition to being timid, I also had a good upbringing, which in Hollywood may make you look snobbish.

Wings in the Dark, my lone Arthur Hornblow production, required Paramount to borrow me. Sadly, it wasn't one of our very best. It may have been a significant story because female transatlantic travelers were common at the time. The studio ultimately decided on melodrama. In a horrible storm that begins over the Atlantic, I played an aviatrix.

My blind ex-boyfriend, Cary Grant, soars up and finds me in the skies. Up until our later photos together, I don't recall much about Cary other than the fact that he was quite gorgeous and busy with his first wife, Virginia Cherrill.

Amelia Earhart was employed by Arthur as a technical adviser, but she was given little to perform. One day, along with her husband, the publisher G. P. Putnam, and the well-known stunt pilot Paul Mantz, we went on a promotional junket to the airport. We ascended and took off. Paul, not Amelia, was the pilot of the aircraft, but throughout, she was incredibly wonderful and pleasant. A few years later, she requested Mantz's companionship for an international flight but was unsuccessful in getting him. She left nonetheless and didn't come back.

My first open cockpit flight was with Paul Mantz. When he first began performing wingovers, the earth would be here half the time and there half the time. My God! I was afraid of dying. However, I was wondering why I didn't fall out, so it was kind of wonderful. It didn't stop me from wanting to learn to fly, but sadly I didn't have the time—or I didn't make the time—to do it. Flying cannot be learned in a single day. Having done so would have required telling Mayer, "I won't do that film!" In those days, Saturdays were days that we worked. They used to work for us on Sundays as well, before the unions declared those to be "golden hours." I never did learn to fly, but I did play many women who did.

Arthur was usually supportive of my career, incredibly compassionate, and interested in me as an actress—even if we only collaborated on that one project. He wasn't a Pygmalion, contrary to popular belief, but he was perceptive and picked up on subtleties I missed. For instance, Adrian frequently utilized those large buttons to trim my clothing in one movie. Myrna, those buttons absolutely erased your face, Arthur replied. That's more significant than it might seem because he recognized that my acting forte is underplaying, which is undermined by an abundance of sophisticated design elements. There is a problem with your gown when someone remarks "What a beautiful gown!" rather than "How nice you look!"

Additionally, Arthur hired a ton of power players, including his attorney Bill Sacks and the agency Myron Selznick, to work for me. Only after Minna Wallis gave her approval did I consent to have Myron represent me. Minna had received support from Myron and his partner Leland Hayward for her own agency. She said, "They're much more significant individuals; they're tops." "You need that kind of representation right now." That was Minna—always thinking about how I would be. She and Arthur were unquestionably correct about Myron Selznick, of course. His brother David told me that he was a fighter and a crack agent because "he has a score to settle." Myron never let them forget how many powerful men had murdered their father, a pioneer of the motion picture industry.

He took over when The Thin Man and my other films were doing exceptionally well at the box office, but for some reason, I had the impression that M-G-M didn't want to do much for me. My 1931 seven-year contract kept me there for more than three more years, though the studio had the right to terminate it at any time. Many people were burned out by such contracts, which is understandable given that I had produced 23 films in less than three years after signing them. They constantly gave you the assurance that if you became famous, they would modify your contract. Well, I had, but it wasn't. They moved me from executive to executive when I requested more money or better working conditions, like the ability to take an occasional holiday.

At that point, my contract paid me roughly $1500 per week, which was half of what they paid Bill Powell and a small portion of what other stars made, and I was required to do more films than any of them. All I wanted was what Bill was getting. They already saw us as a team because I was his co-star and had an equal share of duties. Although $1500 looks like a lot, it was nothing in comparison to the revenue generated by my photographs. I only wanted my fair portion of the gravy; I didn't want anything else.

They rejected Myron's request for these promised changes, and instead cast Bill and myself in Escapade. I argued against being included in that segment, saying, "Don't put me in this stuff. I'm not that melancholy young girl peddling flowers around Vienna's streets. It looked like a poor storyline to me, and I don't believe Bill took it too seriously either. Bill played an artist who finds this waif. Louis B. Mayer then joined in, saying, "Myrna, you're like a member of my family. I couldn't be more sincere if you were my mother, my wife, or my mistress. "My mother, my wife, or my mistress." What a lovely contrast. It was the first time he offered me that song and dance, and it seduced me despite the fact that I knew perfectly well he was only trying to get me to play Escapade. I responded, "Okay, I'll handle it."

My beloved hairstylist Eleanor, whom I had known for years, arrived a week or two into filming in a panic. "You know what they made me do last night? With that fresh Austrian girl, Luise Rainer, I had to do a test, and she performed your role. I questioned, "Oh, did you.. did you really?" She was made to chuckle for comfort while muttering, "Well, that's great for me!"

When Bernie Hyman, one of Mayer's goons, emerged, I had already returned to the set and was back to my regular work. "You want to take a walk?" he beckoned as I approached. We then went for a stroll while he informed me that they were removing me from Escapade and the director, Bob Leonard, was simply standing there with the stomach of a snail. Bernie led me up to the studio manager, an accomplished Irishman named Eddie Mannix, who kept a number of shillelaghs outside his office. I used to grab one whenever I felt like a burger. Therefore, I seized a shillelagh and barged inside. "Oh, God!" Eddie sighed. She is approaching.

He ducked, "Now listen, kid, we made a mistake."
"You have without a doubt—you have no idea what a mistake you have made." Eddie and I were friends, and I liked him, but this annoyed me. I requested that you not put me in the situation in the first place, and when I completed all the prerequisites, you substituted another girl.
We'll just explain that you are ill and go to Palm Springs to rest since we were mistaken.
"No, you won't say anything along those lines. I won't be traveling to Palm Springs because I'm not sick. I left after that.

At supper that night, Arthur, Myron, and I plotted. Myron explained, "You go to the studio in the morning and do what you normally do, makeup, outfit, as if you're going to play the part. You could even need to enter the set. I have no idea, but I believe they will stop you before then. The key is to make sure you have a written release from the photo before you leave the studio.

The following morning, I reported and acted normally. Rainer, she was there and prepared to begin work, and here I was. Of course, she

had nothing to do with this incident, but she appeared terrified and furtive as if she had. Our plan was effective. I told Benny Thau's office over the phone, "Well, I'm here."
The question "You're what?"

"I'm in the studio and ready to work." Benny was usually my studio ally, but this truly placed him in a tough spot. "I don't want any foolishness, and I'm not going to leave Escapade without a release. Nobody is going to say that I'm unwell because I'm not.

Boy! They didn't send that piece of paper at all. I called Myron and told him, "I got it!" This individual was incredibly cunning. He was aware of their plans and knew how to deal with them. You see, they planned to use me as a test case because I was attempting to obtain additional money. I believe they wanted to humiliate me more than they needed another Powell-Loy photo immediately away and actually thought Escapade was a wonderful concept. They weren't getting away with it, to be sure. I wasn't lowering myself. Believe me, I had a chip on my shoulder, and all you had to do was act as though you were going to take it off!

4. THE QUEEN OF THE MOVIES (1936-1942)

We took a car back to Palos Verdes Peninsula after our wedding. Frank Vanderlip, an Italian-loving banker, had rented Villa Narcissa to us. At Portuguese Bend, that magnificent home—a replica of the Villa d'Este—oversaw the water. When the hot, dry Santana winds blew, we took refuge there on the weekends. Oh, those Santana days, when our crowd flocked from Hollywood to escape the heat, bring back such wonderful memories.

When Ernst Lubitsch arrived one weekend, he immediately headed for the water. Ernst ate the leftovers from an oil spill that had occurred at sea. I'll never forget his heavy, hairy figure emerging from the water like some mythical monster covered in this black substance.

Natalie Visart, a designer for Cecil B. De Mille, was brought in by Mitchell Leisen, who directed several of Arthur's Paramount films. She has been one of my best friends through thick and thin; she is bright, humorous, and warm.

Collier Young and Valerie, his first wife, attended the event after traveling from New York. Collie, one of Hollywood's funniest men, later worked as a producer and screenwriter. He also married Joan Fontaine and Ida Lupino. Joan always referred to him as "my favorite ex-husband". But when he first started out as an agent, he had a terrible time making ends meet. Knowing Arthur's fondness for excellent wine, they showed up one weekend with a bottle of an expensive vintage. The Youngs awaited Arthur's ceremonial taste as we sat down at the table and the wine was served. He judged that it was "an agreeable little wine," which totally devastated our visitors. Collie like retelling that tale because, of all, Arthur wasn't just arrogant—he was also mistaken.

Another regular at Villa Narcissa, Eddie Sutherland, was Chaplin's helper in the early silent era. He survived a brief marriage to Louise Brooks and maintained his comedic skills both on and off camera.

Eddie was in love with Loretta Young, a beautiful, vivacious girl. Although they never got married, he claimed to have spent a fortune trying to convince the Vatican to invalidate her prior union.

According to Loretta Young, Eddie Sutherland took me to Myrna and Arthur Hornblow's gorgeous Italian villa on the seashore when they first got married. I was a little afraid since I could still picture that cold, distant creature from our movies, but she gave me a warm welcome and asked, "I suppose you have to go to mass on Sunday?" When I replied "Yes," she made plans to have someone pick me up. The entire weekend was easy and pleasurable for me, yet elegant—beautifully decorated house, lovely service, and delectable food. It established a bar for me. It was noteworthy that Myrna was an excellent hostess in addition to being a talented actor.

She is one of the significant figures in the film industry. She already had a certain quality when she first started, but by the time she joined Metro, she had a lot of experience, and I really enjoyed that aspect of her career. I thought that was extremely elegant. She reached her full potential there because Myrna is one of the few humorous persons in our industry. I refer to true humor. This kind of comprehension or acceptance of relationships, which prominent men and women in those days didn't have, permeated her positions. He was quite masculine, and you played it very feminine, so there was constant confrontation. However, you always had the impression that Myrna would understand it, she thought, no matter how angry she became. She was constantly a touch more learned, sympathetic, and sophisticated. She truly possesses both of those qualities as a person. She has a natural beauty, which for most people would have been sufficient. It was sufficient for Jeanette MacDonald—oh, dear God, assist me. You understand what I mean when I say that Myrna had the first modern-era connection between a man and a woman, especially with William Powell. For all of us, she forged the path.

Recently, Myrna and Clark Gable were in the movie Too Hot to Handle, and she looked just stunning. My mother lamented the fact that fewer films of such kind were being produced. Well, Mama, it seems that they no longer desire photographs like this because otherwise, they would be made, I remarked.

I believe the ones with mental illness are the producers. But how can they truly pull it off once more? The equivalent would be to remark, "This girl will play the Myrna Loy part." You cannot play Myrna Loy without having Myrna Loy's sense of humor and her nose, there is no way! She simply won't be matched by anybody else because she is an original and the first.

Years had passed since I last saw Loretta, but recently, we had dinner at her gorgeous small Beverly Hills home. It was completely adorned by her mother, who is still going strong in her nineties, who also subtly displayed Loretta's Oscar and Emmy awards on the top shelf of the front-hall coat closet. She reasoned that increased exposure would be extravagant and that Loretta wouldn't even move an ashtray that Mama had placed. I was startled to learn that Loretta could recall specifics about those weekends at Villa Narcissa, and we both found the lads' short hunting trip to be amusing.

You know, the Vanderlips raised peacocks that made a tremendous ruckus when they paraded around the estate. Ever heard a peacock call? They scream in the most godforsaken voice possible, a harsh, pungent cry. Those critters played a small game in which they would ascend the stone staircase behind the house, fly, and then land on the roof. You would wait for the roof to cave in on you in the middle of the night when you heard this clump. You had no control over the situation. The Vanderlips revered those creatures as sacred.

Arthur, Eddie, and Jean Negulesco inexplicably vanished from the residence one early morning. They brought a peacock back before lunch. Those devils actually went out and shot one! Absolutely shocked, Loretta and I continued to act like women do, but to no purpose. They transported their kill to the chef at the Bel-Air Country Club in the back of their automobile. According to what they knew, no one had eaten peacock since Nero, but they were going to have it nonetheless. We all went to the Bel-Air and had a peacock at the Vanderlips'. Although it was great, it didn't taste quite like pheasant as I had thought. It had a turkey flavor.

Our bacchanalian celebrations just consisted of roast peacock, an all-girl skinny-dip, and that was it. One hot Santana weekend, the girls decided to slip out for a midnight swim while we had a packed house. Since this was meant to be a private hen celebration, we honestly came prepared with very little to wear. Well, the rascals learned about it, drove over to us in cars, and turned on their headlights. We simply screamed while desperately attempting to cover ourselves in seaweed. Mary Martin alleges that she went to our place for a mixed-gender swimming party. We never did things like that, so if she did, I wasn't there to witness it. Arthur might have continued after I left. As far as I know, no one else in our group did either. We had a fantastic time, but it's absurd that people in Hollywood are so bacchanalian. We overworked ourselves.

Of course, there were always the obvious ones who caused trouble, but not more so than somewhere else. Simply put, certain events become news because of a well-known name. We were aware that there were problematic drinkers, drug users, "great lovers" who preferred boys to females, and "great ladies" who preferred girls to boys, as well as innocent youngsters with an eye on the future. Nobody cared if they kept quiet about it because it was their private matter. In no way did we take pride in it the way they do now. Many girls who eventually rose to fame used to sneak across the border for wild weekends with the Mexican President in exchange for jewels or cash. All they were doing was protecting themselves. The majority of them were young girls who had struggled to succeed. They have since surpassed everything.

In Hidden Valley, at the apex of Coldwater Canyon, we constructed our Hollywood home. I guess we're almost there. Because his bowling alley was improperly designed and the balls continued rolling down the mountain, we knew that Boris Karloff lived someplace above us. Moss Hart jokingly stated that errant bowling balls scared him away from building on the slope between us and Karloff. Sam Goldwyn and the English were highly into the sport at the time.

Coldwater Canyon was made up of untamed, bush-covered slopes and valleys, in spite of bowling balls and being close to Beverly slopes. When we first began construction, the only indication of civilization was the winding, white macadamized road that ascended our hill. A large clapboard house that combines Colonial beauty with the contemporary freedom we desired was designed by our architect. We constructed tennis courts, a pool, and a pool house with changing rooms and a bar underneath the house on a different level. We had a beautiful lime orchard below that, in the valley floor, where Jim, our gardener, once caught a persistent fan removing a tree for a memento. And we cultivated gardens everywhere. Oh, how beautiful the blossoms were! I feel horrible just thinking about what I put there. Arthur and I were making a combined yearly salary of almost $300,000, and trust me, we lived up to it. I'm awful with money. Awful! My funds were always taken care of by others. All I had to do was earn money, which they would deposit in the bank, after which Arthur and I would spend it. However, we enjoyed ourselves. It was valuable.

According to Betty Black, I once drove up to Myrna's house in the spring, and it was the most breathtaking scene I had ever seen. A huge hill of wildflower seeds that led to her house had just been scattered by the gardener. They were of every variety and color. It was a very well-run estate, exactly how Arthur wanted it to be, modeled after English grand homes. Everything had to be very English, including his friends, his clothes, and even the way Myrna dressed after he started studying her every move. Myrna never gave those matters any thought, but Arthur, who was twelve years older and more traditional, did. Like Gene Markey later on, he desired to lead a millionaire's lifestyle.

My mother commented on Myrna's home the first time she saw it, "Gosh, she must have to work awfully hard to support all these people." They occasionally employed up to seven gardeners at once. They employed a butler, live-in maids, a laundry attendant who also served as Arthur's valet, a German chauffeur by the name of Helmut, and a fantastic Russian chef by the name of Sergei. Everyone in Hollywood who was fortunate enough to be invited talked about the meal they served.

Except for Bob and me, Arthur was a snob to all of Myrna's old acquaintances and the center of her social life. Probably since Bob was an officer, he liked us. That was Arthur's Britishness. Since Della was Myrna's mother and Myrna was still somewhat under her influence—you don't just break away—he would occasionally invite Della and Auntie around. Myrna purchased a car for her, employed a maid and a chauffeur, and Arthur often delivered items to her home. However, Myrna and Arthur's marriage was never centered around a family. The Laughtons, the Nigel Bruces, Louis Bromfield, Alfred Hitchcock, the Goldwyns, and the Selznicks were among the authors and composers who were always from New York or who were well-known in Hollywood and the British colonies. Tennis was played, there were those people around all the time, and Sergei and his wife produced magnificent buffets.

Bob and David Niven, who wasn't all that well recognized at the time, played doubles one day. But Myrna foresaw his destiny. He's a darn fine actor, and she believes he'll succeed. After the game, I was enjoying my conversation with him when Gene Markey and his wife, Hedy Lamarr, came. Bob was a huge fan of Hedy Lamarr. I was charmed by Gene and have always been. Later, when Myrna was married to Gene, I got to know him very well. He was also writing at the time in addition to drawing, and I had read and praised his novels to him. I never felt in awe of these folks because they were famous—they were always very courteous to me—but rather because of the knowledge and discourse they shared. Myrna had no time for those who went out every night to party. At Myrna's place, you had to be on your game.

There was a diverse population of creative individuals everywhere. Everyone was employed and engaged in some form of activity. Other than when they had time off, which wasn't frequently, people didn't just sit around. There was so much wit and enthusiasm. These individuals and the environment they came from influenced the type of smart humor I produced for movies. They studied the so-called leisure class, the ruling class at the time, and expertly reenacted it. There was a formal manner of life back then, with wealthy people alike Noel Coward having butlers and maids. It doesn't currently, at least not in that way, hence it isn't being written about. These days, life is a bit more depressing. Being clever is quite challenging. I was familiar with people who spoke that way, including Noel himself, who frequently stopped by my set when he visited Hollywood, Herman Mankiewicz, Moss Hart, George Kaufman, Dorothy Parker, and Arthur, who wasn't exactly a slouch either. In reality, it used to be quite difficult. At the end of a conversation, I'd be worn out. I would sit there and consider when I would come up with a clever comment.

Along with Dorothy Parker, Harry Kurnitz was one of the great wits, but unlike her, he never turned his humor against himself. Long before he composed I Love You Again or Shadow of the Thin Man for Bill and me, Collier and Valerie Young came to my place, and we hit it off right away. One night, we all went to a wild, wild party; it seems that we all consumed enough alcohol, and Harry consumed more than enough. The following day, he showed up at our place for a scheduled tennis match looking utterly hopeless. He moaned, "I want a record of how I feel right now. "I'm going to put it in a time capsule to demonstrate what modern man was like to the world in many years from now."

Tennis matches were played in our house, which grew into a popular gathering spot, even while I was at work. Our courts were carved directly from the mountain, leaving behind dirt and vegetation that gardeners continued to trim back. One day, someone yelled as Arthur and my brother David were playing doubles. A rattlesnake was slithering along the court's wall. We hurried back to where David was holding the snake down with his tennis racket after I went for Jim, the gardener, who was usually killing those critters. One bite from one of them will kill you, but David simply held the bloody beast down until Jim killed it. I thought my little brother was being really brave by doing that.

I'm afraid David wasn't there too much because Arthur treated my family with a lot of snobbery. He had no excuse to be upset simply because he was born on the West Side of New York and had finally made it to the East Side. It wasn't quite pleasant for Mother and Aunt Lou when I invited them to dinner. But with all of my spouses, my mother was always on his side. After a disagreement with Arthur one evening, I walked down to her place. "You can't stay here," she commanded. "Go back home to your husband." She refused to tolerate me. After that, I had a lot of issues with him, but I never went to Mother.

After Arthur acquired a vicious black police dog that terrified the living daylights out of me, the rattlesnakes had some competition. Why on earth are you bringing that breed of dog into this home? I questioned, but Arthur did not let me. One afternoon, Sidney Howard, who had traveled from New York to write the Gone With the Wind script, and I were conversing happily on the veranda when all of a sudden, Arthur ran for his life toward the driveway with this dog chasing after him. Sidney and I were frightened, helpless, and unsure of what to do. As usual, I finally called Jim, and together we pursued them down the drive: Jim, the gardener, Sidney Howard, and I were running madly in the back, making it appear as though a Mack Sennett pursuit was taking place while Arthur pursued the growling black dog at his heels. Arthur wasn't attacked when we got down the bottom, but that police dog wasn't there for very long.

Arthur had a knack for drawing in amusing and interesting people. Charlie Chaplin and I had first met at one of the De Milles' gatherings, but he didn't visit us until he and Arthur had gotten together somewhere. Many people avoided him since he was a very self-absorbed man who wasn't very interested in anything that didn't involve him or his work: "My God! Is he just coming to bug you? You won't get any sleep, so be careful. It is real. I found him fascinating even though he would talk into the night. He spoke for a while, enjoying the limelight and sharing fascinating tales about events that occurred on his sets. He would describe the evolution of his routines while playing out each step as if he were directing a scene. He was acutely aware of the process. You seen this creative process in action and understood how those outstanding films developed.

He once spent hours talking in our library before I finally had to excuse myself, hoping he would realize that I had to go. I said, "I have to work tomorrow and you know what it means to get up at five-thirty." God knows exactly when that was. Although Charlie was still surrounded by rapt listeners, I will never forget how perplexed and slightly insulted he appeared. Nothing could possibly be more important than his performance, in his opinion.

Another enthralling raconteur with a twist was Reginald Gardiner. He could be anything he wanted to be thanks to his expressive voice and deft hands. You could literally see rolls of repetitive patterns in his stunning wallpaper. He made the usually boring train ride from New York to Hollywood more enjoyable when we took it together. We exited the vehicle at Albuquerque in order to get some fresh air and stroll up to the engine. Steam engines made all those great noises back then as they went shshshsh. Reggie personified the engine, saying "This engine is livid," "absolutely livid," before executing a flawless copy.

Hedy Lamarr was with Reggie when I first met her. She frequently opined that he was the man she ought to have wed. Reggie was sort of carrying her around because she had sprained her ankle, but you couldn't help but notice that stunning face of hers. Oh, that was fantastic—truly fantastic! People seem to think Hedy is a blank, allegedly due to her beauty. In no way. When I knew her, she was always charming and had a good sense of humor. She joined the group that used to visit my house when she wed Gene Markey.

At Paramount, Arthur produced a number of musicals, which put him in contact with the New York-based composers. They started congregating at our house. I owned a lovely medium grand Steinway piano that was built of pearwood. My mother was always quite particular about pianos; she would only ever touch a Steinway. One evening, Richard Rodgers, Jerome Kern, George, and Ira Gershwin wrestled over the piano, nearly knocking one another over. When one stood up, another jumped in. They kept having fun. There was Mexican composer Augustine Lara. He watched this show of musical prowess in complete awe. The talent, dear God! But back then, we actually had a musical theater.

Dick Rodgers played the piano beautifully, something that composers don't always do. We had met while recording Love Me Tonight and remained close friends ever since. When they would travel to California, I would invariably run into him and Dorothy.

Aside from the wonderful Love Me Tonight soundtrack, he also composed a song for Manhattan Melodrama, which Larry Hart later changed the words to make into "Blue Moon," a quintessentially New York song. It has an appearance similar to a city at night. At my house, he performed those and other songs, always his own tunes, of course, competing with his friends for the use of the pearwood piano.

While composing that beautiful score for High, Wide and Handsome, one of Arthur's Paramount musicals, Jerry Kern entered my life. He was sweet, little, and had a cheeky sense of humor. I loved the man. He occasionally sat on our front porch when I returned from the studio in the evening. From his home in Beverly Hills, he would drive up and wait for us. He once got locked inside a huge porcelain jar on the porch while trying to surprise me. We had a terrible time getting him out. We had to tug, coax, and pressure that hefty object as Arthur and I, together with a few of the servants, overturned it, almost shattering his little bones in the process. This was Jerry, full of silly jokes to counteract what seemed like an endless stream of inventiveness. He stayed up late working, which was difficult for his attractive wife who had to be patient because they were all married to those crazy men. One night, a bird's persistent call irritated him as he tried to concentrate beside an open window. He yelled to his wife, "Close that window!" "I'm going crazy over it," But the bird call kept coming back to him, and after being turned into dozens of songs, it was transformed into the opening notes of "I've Told Every Little Star." From him, lovely tunes gushed forth.

That memorable evening in Hidden Valley, George Gershwin eventually found himself at the piano. You know, George never wanted to sleep. People started to depart as he simply continued to play. Only the two of us were eventually left in my living room. At four in the morning, he was still playing the piano. I was never really able to understand George. Naturally, I didn't interact with him as much as I did with Dick and Jerry, but I did spend time with him and enjoy his music. He had a passion about him, but he played rather than said much. Music was his true love. I don't recall what he said or played during that extended session at my residence. It was extremely unusual since a week later, he passed away from a brain tumor. He may not have been aware of it that evening, but the tragic death brought to light the irony of the final song he had performed, "They Can't Take That Away from Me."

John T. Hornblow, Terry's son Arthur, is the most cherished memory of all the individuals from those times. He was hardly more than six when his father first introduced us, and he almost toppled over in his low bow. I loved him immediately after that. Since I was Arthur's nickname for me, he wrote: "Dear Minnie," when he got back to his mother in Warrenton, Virginia: "I am sorry I went away from you." It was a huge love affair from the outset.

During his summer visits, he was frequently accompanied by a nurse or his French governess, and we frequently had infant animals around. We went through everything one does with kids, and he joined boys' clubs and fractured his arm. His father, who hadn't spent much time with him, attempted to make up for it by imposing a schedule of activities but abstaining from actual participation. I made an effort to fill Arthur's shoes by bringing him speckled bass fishing on those excursion boats off the Malibu pier. I had a friendship with Terry. We cooperate on projects. Arthur planned and I played at the parties we threw for him with the sons of David and Irene Selznick, Steve Broidy, Buff Cobb, and other famous youngsters. Every kind of kid-friendly activity would be available, including gunny-sack races. They returned home with the appearance of having been through a war. I did too.

Naturally, I spent most of my time at work. I'd take him to the studio in the morning so he could see more of Terry. He cherished talking to Helmut on the tiny microphone from the rear seat while Hawaiian music played on the car radio. He periodically came to the studio to see me work or to take a tour. After lunch in the commissary, Helmut would then drive him home.

Those who measure these things refer to the latter five years of that decade as my "golden years." They were undoubtedly productive years. I did twenty films between 1934's The Thin Man and 1939's Another Thin Man. Although their quality varied, each carried the mark of professionals and artists coming together to produce mass entertainment. A movie can never again be what television is to the general population now. The idea that so much high-caliber content emerged from what were effectively entertainment factories is truly astonishing.

One of the best "screwball comedies" was "Libeled Lady", which featured a fantastic cast and fast-paced direction from Jack Conway. Bill Powell and I typically played independently from Jean Harlow and Spencer Tracy, so we didn't collaborate with them very much on that film. Since it was our first time working together since my marriage, Spence continued throughout the shooting. He walked around whining and acting like a suitor who had been wronged. In the commissary, he set up a "hate Hornblow table" and declared that only the men I had rejected were allowed to sit there. So all these guys who were supposed to have crushes on me but didn't at all joined him. Even though it was merely a joke, Spence got his point across.

Bill and I, along with the adorable actor who played my father, Walter Connolly, traveled to the mountains of California for the exterior shots. The amazing fishing scene where Bill makes every mistake and catches the prize fish was filmed there. I scream as I see it now. It's a hilarious piece of work, but Bill was a highly talented man who was capable of great humor and tragedy, as well as everything else.

The only time Arthur ever accompanied me on location, we went up there. Fortunately, Bill liked him, and they grew to be close friends. Living in tiny cabins with a chuck wagon to provide food for the employees and ourselves, we stayed there for about a week. The studios started using those chuck wagons, a relic of the Old West, out in the field. The cuisine was excellent, possibly similar to what my father had prepared during a roundup over a campfire. The scenery was stunning up in the mountains, with spectacular sunsets, long, tranquil nights, and a nice change from cramped sound stages.

Irvin S. Cobb forewarned me that "a sequel is like a second helping of casaba." With After the Thin Man, we had luck. Dashiell Hammett created an original story that continued the plot of the first, which the Hacketts once more adapted for the big screen. Bill and I reprised our roles as Nick and Nora with Asta in tow, while Hunt Stromberg served as the film's producer and director. Jimmy Stewart performed admirably as the insane offender in one of his first acting performances. He proclaimed, "I'm going to marry Myrna Loy!" while dashing around with his camera and taking shots of everyone on the set. He was incredibly excited and passionate about everything.

I boarded the train with Bill and Jean Harlow since we were shooting exteriors in San Francisco. He had managed to whisk her away from her mother, even if she wasn't visible in the image. She had such a strong hold over that girl. Unofficially engaged, Bill had given Jean a huge star-sapphire ring, which she exhibited with pride as they rode the train. Bill continued making comments about how it was really too big, but Jean was ecstatic. She treasured this very much. During that journey, I came to see how utterly childish and full of the energy and wonder that defined her was her love for Bill. She was ready to get married, but he was hesitant. Naturally, he felt extremely guilty about it after she passed away. He adored her, but his previous marriage to a woman in New York, as well as his most recent union with Carole Lombard, both ended in divorce.

They had booked Bill and I into the Flyshaker Suite at the St. Francis in San Francisco. The administration assumed we were wed. After only five photos together, they already regarded us as a pair! Naturally, it was hysterical. Jean was here, but with the press closing in on us, we couldn't be overt about the situation. Convention attendees had already occupied every accommodation other than a tiny hallway bedroom downstairs, further complicating matters. I was at a loss for what to do, but Jean was fantastic. Nothing needs to be done, she said. Bill will just have to go downstairs, I guess. I don't know how horrible his room was because I never saw it, but Bill was complaining vehemently and desperately trying to move upstairs, to tell you the truth.

I gained one of my most treasured friendships as a result of the mix-up. Jean and I had so much fun, you'd think we were in boarding school. We would converse and drink gin into the wee hours of the morning, occasionally laughing and occasionally debating more serious topics. She discussed Paul Bern, the Metro executive who committed suicide while they were still married. After four years, she was still very much thinking about that. Because she loved him, she told me what a horrific experience that had been. She got involved with him because he never treated her like a sex symbol but rather treated her like a woman. He also exhibited care and consideration. She detailed everything to me. She did not explicitly state to me that he could not complete the marriage. How do you say anything like that, then? However, I figured it was his issue, which was probably made worse by her attractive appearance, as I could detect some remorse in her response—there had to be in a circumstance like that. However, the overwhelming emotion was love, along with a lot of adoration and understanding of his shortcomings. She partially blamed that sexy image for the fact that he couldn't stand to let her down.

People's personalities and the roles they performed were never muddled, as so many of these wannabe biographers tend to do. Although Jean was always upbeat and entertaining, she also had a lot of self-respect and was a very sensitive person. All of that additional information was fake. She was not at all like that. She was just a talented actress who portrayed a vivacious persona with sex appeal. I can assure you that it is not enjoyable to be a sexpot. Because of my brief employment in that department and the fact that I always had one foot in the door, I didn't have as much difficulty as others of them had. My God! Take a look at Marilyn Monroe when you consider what this nation does to those ladies! I suppose being sexy is wrong, but it's acceptable for people to drool in the public eye vicariously. This subversive lewdness must have its roots in our puritanical past. I have no idea, but I'm glad I wasn't a sexpot. All the sexpots have already died or are soon to.

Do you recall that dreadful book about Jean that was written? That is characteristic of the biography school that tries to match truth to image. She allegedly drove around San Francisco after drinking too much and sleeping with cab drivers. For the love of God, she was on set with Bill or myself when we were working. Oh, the waste of paper that is printed drives me crazy! Believe me, much of it is garbage, but the worst part is that people actually believe what they read. There is some sort of holiness to the printed word. Even thinking about the book that Joan Crawford's daughter authored makes me feel sick, so I can't talk about it. I've known Joan for 50 years, and the Joan I knew wasn't like that. Why do people not think about the source? I saw Christina's mind at work and how it functions. The daughter of Margaret Sullavan published a book that is as terrible. Maggie forfeited her prime professional years to care for those kids, and now she receives it. And I'm enraged by these supposedly secret lifestyles. Previously, only the Police Gazette published that information. The rule of sensationalism at all costs appears to be under attack right now, almost with a demonic zeal. Consider referring to Errol Flynn as a Nazi spy. My God! He never stayed sober for long enough. How are these things printed? I was recently claimed by a bird in Toronto to have been recruited as an American spy during World War II. What a moron! I worked for the Red Cross throughout the war in Washington and New York. They want what from us? They're genuinely enjoying themselves as they tear apart everyone they ever liked.

We put forth a ton of effort at that San Francisco location. With roughly sixty principals, crew, and hundreds of local extras, we filmed all over the city; however, Woody Van Dyke always preferred a merry group, so there were plenty of parties. Jean had a tendency to get weary easily, and in the morning, her typically snow-white skin occasionally seemed slate-gray. She seemed like a sick girl to me. I got in touch with Saxton Pope, a friend of mine who works at the University of California Medical Center in San Francisco, as I was aware of how difficult it was to remove Jean from her devoted Christian Scientist mother. I never had checks in Los Angeles; I always went to him. The columnists would report that if you were a movie star and went into a hospital there, you were having an abortion or a baby. They immediately pursue you. I continue to be very quiet about my diseases because of this. They are goblins. The obituaries are currently being dusted off if I go in for a checkup right now.

I gave Saxton and Jeanne an invitation to a cocktail event at St. Francis. I advised him to have a good look at the female. In addition to your interest in her, which you will undoubtedly have, look into her health. In order to flirt with her, he claimed, "I'm a doctor," and he fiddled around while taking her pulse. She didn't notice. Even though he was at a party and unable to make a diagnosis, he subsequently remarked, "When I took hold of that girl's wrist, it was almost like the veins were hardening." As I recall, he speculated that she had a blood issue as a youngster, which may have contributed to her skin's extreme whiteness. I made her promise me there and then that she would return there for a comprehensive checkup since he wanted to give her a thorough examination. Even though I set up an appointment at the medical center, she never decided to go. She made friends with the Popes and persuaded them to reconsider. Jean has a lot of persuasive power.

Let's be clear about my next image for a moment. Regardless of what the detractors and commentators may say about Parnell, I like it. In the title character, I believe Clark Gable is fantastic, and I enjoy Katie O'Shea. That movie contains the best love scene he has ever performed. When Parnell and Katie first meet, he mentions seeing her at the opera wearing a white dress. It's a lovely scene. The beginning of the love that would upend the British Empire is palpable.

It seems that the issue was Clark's somber, persistent performance as Parnell. People didn't want to be reminded that he was an actor because he had been so stereotyped as those red-blooded Blackie Nortons. They focused on masculine content. And I was breezy Nora Charles, which prevented me from dressing as Adrian in the finery of the nineteenth century and developing a more serious persona. Thousands of irate fans wrote to the studio back then—that was the norm. Some of the critics claimed that we played outside of our comfort zone. For goodness' sake, we were actors. We couldn't always act like Blackie Norton and Nora Charles. It's interesting that Joan Crawford was originally slated to play Katie O'Shea, while I was set to star alongside Bill Powell and Bob Montgomery in The Last of Mrs. Cheyney. Because Joan's earlier attempt at a nineteenth-century portrayal, The Gorgeous Hussy, met with the same level of audience backlash, they abruptly switched us. So many of us, including Clark, Joan, and I, were the victims of our carefully cultivated perceptions.

The fact that we were pitted against so many foul-weather English performers in Parnell—those veddy British character actors with their agonizingly accurate West End accents—didn't help the situation. Even when up against Edna May Oliver, who wasn't English but might as well have been, my sort of mid-Atlantic accent held up quite well. She was a wonderful woman who was very funny and a devout Yankee spinster living in a small house in Westwood. The contrast, however, worked against Clark because he was the last person in the world to attempt an English accent. It wasn't done on purpose. These British performers, including Edmund Gwenn, Donald Crisp, and Alan Marshall, were wonderful, giving people. In fact, while filming in front of a miniature House of Commons, we related a spectacular episode. Work was suspended, a radio was made, and the British contingent got together to hear Edward VIII's speech announcing his abdication. They were all appalled by his choice and protested strongly, believing it to be a grave error, while the gloomy, gray Parliament set loomed behind us, accentuating that poignant historical moment.

I find it really difficult to comprehend the widespread opposition to Parnell. Even though it was written by John Van Druten and S.N. Behrman, the script does not completely ignore historical events. It went deeper than the majority of the so-called historical dramas into topics like Home Rule. Metro worked hard to be precise. An arrogant young Randolph Churchill argued that Gladstone would have been addressed as "Mr. Prime Minister" in the House of Commons when he visited the set. Our director, John Stahl, halted the action so that the research team could cable the Clerk of the House to confirm that "Mr. Gladstone" was really legitimate in 1887. Parnell was not the disastrous failure that history has painted it to be. Contrary to the common misconception, it received high marks from many reviewers at the time and turned a fair profit. No doubt, it didn't diminish our standing. In the largest-ever nationwide poll, Clark and I were chosen as King and Queen of the Movies at the time of our film's premiere.

Because Aunt Lou slipped a 1937 New York Daily News into an old scrapbook, I can tell you the specifics of that thing. That faded relic indicates that almost twenty million individuals were surveyed for the results by fifty-three newspapers in the major cities of the United States and Canada. Even for a formal coronation, Ed Sullivan traveled to Hollywood with these tin and purple velvet crowns. After that, Clark would constantly refer to me as "Queenie," which had a Western saloon vibe to it. The entire situation was screaming. Bill Powell, who finished fourth in the men's category, sent me a box from a florist that was the size of a couch and was full of resentment. The message on the card was, "With Love from William IV." We didn't take any of that seriously, and neither did the box office rankings that consistently put us in the top ten over those years. Funny, but those laws and titles didn't have the same significance for us as you might think. We went to M-G-M together, and it seemed like Clark and I were two teenagers trying to make out. While we were learning our trade and taking our work seriously, we were also having a great time. Later on, Clark remarked, "We never expected to be legends."

We may have understood that this legendary nonsense was an unavoidable outcome of all the exposure if we had given it some thought. Because there were so many newspapers back then, interviews resembled presidential press conferences, as I've already stated. You needed assistance from a studio member at all times to get you through them. My guardian was Larry Barbier, one of Howard Strickling's subordinates. Larry would travel with me whenever I had studio business in New York or elsewhere, and once we got there, local Metro staff would join us. I would always be surrounded by a phalanx of guards. The studio treated us like royalty. Judy Garland and I used to talk about the "M-G-M syndrome" as a peculiar form of conditioning that wasn't good for us. I thought it was wonderful fun to shake them and get away from the continual watch. Some people, like Judy, were overly reliant on it. However, you also had to deal with the general populace, as I rudely learned while traveling to New York with Arthur.

Like all native New Yorkers, Arthur enjoyed shopping there, and back then, when suburban malls and cheap chain stores didn't exist, New York shops were truly special. One morning, we went to Macy's to buy placemats and other household items. A salesgirl brought me behind her exhibit to show me what they had because I'm a fairly quick shopper and don't mess around. As I'm looking through this things, suddenly a sea of faces suddenly encroaches on me. Word has gotten out that you are in the store, so we need to get you out of here, say two large Macy officers as they approach, grab my arms, and begin pulling me. They are ascending the stairs and elevators. They had a mob on their hands, and they were terrified. I luv you!, a woman shouts just then. "I luv you!" she exclaims, giving me a neck crack. I did in fact see stars. My life was almost taken by her luf. These two officers lead me downstairs as I stagger and shout for Arthur, who has walked off to another department, while yelling at me in a heartbreaking tone, "Don't you know better than to do such a thing? Never enter this building again. They basically threw me out of Macy's after guiding me to a side door. Imagine! I remained motionless until Arthur came across me. I exclaimed, "They just threw me out." They truly warned me not to return, I mean. We started giggling at the absurdity as we walked toward Fifth Avenue to have a brandy shot.

To return to my friendship with Clark Gable, I should mention that it was odd given how it had begun. We grew to love one another. He was already in love with Carole Lombard at the time, therefore we weren't lovers. In fact, after I thwarted his initial assault, we became closer to being siblings. Nobody thinks that, and it's easy to see why when you think about Lou MacFarlane's remark after I pushed him off the porch: "I wouldn't care if he couldn't read." Clark's impact on women was like that. But we had a special bond. Oh, when people were watching, he occasionally gave me the macho routine, but when we were by ourselves, he changed.

At the conclusion of a photograph, we used to always celebrate together. It was Clark's insistence. The director might be included, or might not. We simply had a ritual of sorts between the two of us. He would read me poetry, generally Shakespearean sonnets, as we shared a bottle of champagne. He read poetry brilliantly and sensitively, and he loved it, but he wouldn't dare tell anyone else. He feared that if he appeared weak or effeminate, people would mistake him for the tough guy who enjoyed hunting and fishing. He just placed his trust in me. I'm about to reveal something about him that he never wanted me to, but I never brought it up when he was still living.

He had to maintain his manly demeanor in front of Carole. Even though she made fun of and mocked him about it, he still had to show it to her. Although Carole was attractive and feminine, he would simply sit back and howl if she started sweating profusely or took off like a stevedore. It pushed him, but he enjoyed it. That might be the reason he attracted older women in general. He had two older wives in the past. They obviously aided him; one was a theater teacher and the other was a wealthy Texan. Clark, however, wouldn't wed for those reasons since he was too independent. He may have simply felt less under pressure from them. He basically kept doing that all his life. He used to see Dolly O'Brien, who was a lot older after Carole passed away. Even though I was younger, I think he associated me with being a mother because he had some sort of obsession with mothers.

He was cursed by the ugly macho thing that exists in our country. He was constantly being reminded that he needed to do this action. Nobody, least of all Clark, understood that he was a pretty excellent actor by chance. Oh, he wanted to be an actor, but he constantly mocked his talent and pretended that it was irrelevant. He was actually a bashful man who harbored a dreadful sense of inadequacy. He could have done things, but something was missing that prevented him from accomplishing them. He has a line in Test Pilot where he mentioned the sky as the girl in the blue dress. He was so horrified by that scene that he passed out. When we shot it, he became so distressed that I had to keep calming and consoling him. He performed the part flawlessly, so it wasn't that he couldn't, but he was concerned that it would give him a soft appearance. He couldn't get out of the macho contraption that was tied to him.

After Parnell, Clark stopped challenging his audience; even Rhett Butler exhibited the traits that everyone had come to expect of him. He eventually came to the conclusion that was all he could do, and upholding his macho persona to the last end bothered him. He was far past the age at which he should have been roping and getting pulled around by all those horses in The Misfits when it finally killed him. Do you know the only issue we had with Clark playing Parnell? nobody would think he could die of a heart attack while playing the part. Ironically, it is exactly what actually occurred.

Movie people were too busy establishing themselves during my formative years in the studios to give social conscience any thought. I once questioned, "Why does every Black person in a movie play a servant? What about merely a black individual holding a briefcase as they ascend the steps of a courthouse? Well! the storm it brought about! It was at the start of the 1930s. But later in the decade, largely as a result of the political initiatives of transplanted New Yorkers, Hollywood started to acknowledge the rest of the world. Dash Hammett served as head of the Motion Picture Artists Committee, which invited Ernest Hemingway to a benefit in order to raise money for the Spanish Loyalists. Hemingway gave a speech and screened The Spanish Earth, a powerful anti-Fascist film he composed and narrated that helped fund 18 ambulances and a variety of medical supplies. Many performers, including Bob Montgomery, who was terrified he'd never get over it when he became an Eisenhower Republican, put their names on ambulances. I have no idea what transpired. He had always remained so devoted to F.D.R. I used to make fun of Bob's switch by saying, "You look more and more like a Republican every day."

Hemingway practically reigned as king, reveling in the attention and money that everyone showed him. While Bill Powell and I were filming Double Wedding, he came to the set to solicit, but he was more interested in alcohol than donations. While Bill went to get a bottle, Hemingway stayed out all afternoon. Although he and Bill had a great time getting roaring drunk, we needed to take a picture. With Martha Gellhorn, whom he eventually married, Hemingway was traveling. Both then and subsequently, when I saw more of her in Italy, she left an impression on me as a woman of substance. However, the great man struck me as more of a washout because he was typically intoxicated, loud, and self-important.

I'll admit that at Double Wedding, I wasn't at my best. It was harder to make than most of my comedies and included more slapstick. In a trailer with two sides missing and numerous people crammed inside and around it, we spent three weeks filming. Despite the possibility that I never saw the image, I despised it. Possibly because Jean Harlow's passing occurred while the movie was being made, Bill and I were left in utter anguish. Oh, that was terrible, a terrible blow; I had a great affection for Jean. I experienced a dreadful combination of grief, shame, and irritability since I was powerless to do what might have saved her: remove her from her mother so that a doctor could examine her. That woman is to blame for Jean's demise, in my opinion. The cerebral edema that ultimately led to her death could have been prevented in a 26-year-old girl with the right care.

Bill and I attempted to continue this slapstick comedy, but he passed out and the film kept getting pushed back. He held himself responsible for Jean's passing because he had loved her but never wed her and separated her from her mother. When he fell down, he would call me for support. He cried into the phone one day, "This is a good throat-cutting day." He had already moved on by the time I arrived, so I put on my hat and fled. "It was an Irish funk," he said. Just the Irish in me, I guess.

Man-Proof went more easily. We had a fantastic cast, and I had a unique role with a great drunk scene—or so everyone said). Roz Russell's on-screen love interest, Walter Pidgeon, was always a delight. Over a forty-year period, Pidge and I were able to collaborate once or twice every ten years. And that was the only time I ever worked with the handsome Franchot Tone, who I regrettably never got to know very well. The marriage between him and Joan Crawford wasn't going well at the moment. He slept a lot on the shoot, as I recall. He slept all the time.

Roz was being the vivacious, joyous person she always is. Despite all the studio crap about pitting her against me, we ended up becoming friends while shooting the picture. She had really interesting parties and lived down the hill from me. She frequently made jokes about receiving my rejects at her events. She would comment that the covers of all of the scripts had your name wiped out. When you force them out of your home after waiting until it is dark, they roll down the hill and crash against my front door. They are portrayed in that way. To get rid of you, I'd like to ship you throughout the globe. I wrote her a card when Arthur and I were in Scandinavia and said, "Well, you've succeeded. Halfway around the world, I am. I have little doubt that Roz would have enjoyed a number of the roles I portrayed. At Metro, they didn't always employ her effectively and occasionally overlooked stuff. It was challenging to predict what people would achieve. She periodically got better jobs because of my rejections, but she didn't really earn her big breaks there. She surely recovered well after that.

One of M-G-M's hit movies, Test Pilot, is a personal favorite of mine. The writing, directing, shooting, technological know-how, and casting of that faultless stock business truly serve as examples of what big-studio filmmaking may be like. Imagine starring in a movie alongside Lionel Barrymore, Spencer Tracy, and Clark Gable! What actress would not look attractive? We only got a few quick sequences together and a beautiful phone discussion that we both recorded separately, which was a shame because I adored Lionel. His sequences were scripted for a seated position because of how much his crippled leg troubled him. He appeared happy, which was understandable given how lavishly we all treated him—especially Clark and Spence, who both held Lionel in high regard.

As I've already mentioned, I portrayed Clark as a strong, independent woman. When people were observing, he always sought to make me the center of attention. Despite our pleasant poetry sessions, there was always a constant competition, and I was typically quite combative with him. Writers for Metro picked up on this and adapted our images accordingly. I didn't mind because it made my portions a little bit more varied. In the wonderful porch scene from Test Pilot, I sexually entice him without so much as brushing hands.

I always got along well with Spencer Tracy. We used the same method. Naturally, I was unaware of it at the time because people didn't think about such things. We didn't think critically. But after reflecting on what we actually did, I came to understand that it applied to both Spence and I. He was meticulous and conscious of what he performed with each part. Those performances, which gave the impression of being unhurried and carefree, were meticulously planned and organized. He was always so terrified of going too far, even though he was aware that in movies you had to keep your distance. He was good in part because of that.

He wouldn't let me leave while he was doing retakes. He'd say, "No, no, you wait." You must let me know how I'm doing. He would act out the event and then quickly ask, "Did I ham it up? Have I gone too far?

Sometimes, even though it wasn't true, I would respond "Yes," just because he seemed to be seeking the challenge. He had a lot of stuff, and it was difficult to resist, so it's also possible that I was reacting to it. He would repeat the scene as a result. Naturally, it would be wonderful, but I would say, "That one's O.K., that's all right." And he'd take me at my word. He never understood. As far as Spence was concerned, I could do no wrong.

Although Spence and Clark weren't the best of friends off the set, they loved each other and got along well. They engaged in a spirited conversation during filming—something that truly hardly ever happened with many individuals. As I've already mentioned, Clark called me "Queenie"; he went by "the King," Spence went by "the Iron Duke," and our director Victor Fleming went by "the Monk" for whatever reason I can no longer recall. Their rivalry had a certain sharpness since Spence sought Clark's status as an actor and Clark coveted Spence's stature with the public and the studio. Spence would address Clark as "Your Majesty" following our intended coronation. When Clark called Spence a Wisconsin ham, Spence would respond, "What about Parnell?" It was just macho vs macho, but when we went to the location at March Field in Riverside, things got a little out of hand.

We were enjoying a casual lunch with several of the officers after spending the morning filming exteriors around the airfield. They planned to use one of the large Air Corps bombers we were utilizing in the image to transport Clark, Spence, and Victor to Catalina. Spence was heard saying, "Thank you very much, but I don't want to go." I observed that the flyers appeared to get what he was talking about, but Gable and Fleming immediately attacked him and berated him for not attending. You're aware of how males are. While Spence sat there, they made all kinds of insulting jokes. I was enraged, but since I hadn't heard the buildup, I refrained from saying anything.

Spence sprang up from the table as soon as the others departed, grabbed me, and we immediately fled. I enquired, "What's the matter?" "What is happening here?" He declined to respond. He simply dragged me across the field while tightly holding onto my arms till we arrived at the vehicle that took us to and from Riverside. He finally spoke it out loud on the drive home, saying, "Well, Goddamn it, you know what would happen if I went with them. They'll head straight for a bar as soon as they step off the plane. I can't do that, as you well know. Then it finally hit me. He was worried about becoming wasted. He had a long history of drinking issues, and just one drink would set him off. Although he was aware that it was a serious issue, he had the self-control to refrain from shooting. Sometimes, in between shots, he would simply vanish for a moment, but not while he was working. This was something that Gable and Fleming didn't grasp—more accurately, they refused to understand and just kept berating him. Spence had sat there and accepted it in front of all those men rather than take the chance of relapsing. He said angrily, "You know I can't do that," as they drove to Riverside. Yes, sweetheart, I know you can't do that, I attempted to reassure him. Now, calm down. Calm down. He was so furious that I made the decision there and then to always keep an eye on him.

The odd old Riverside Inn, with its caves, cataracts, and musty charm, was where we were staying. I said, "Look, why don't we have an early dinner," intending to keep him safe. Before the others return, let's eat. I told Shirley Hughes about it. He used to phone her frequently in an effort to locate me, and they eventually became friends. By this point, he had, sort of, quit doing that; nonetheless, I wasn't having too much trouble with him. We simply settled into a close friendship, but he continued to hold onto and have faith in me. He knew I would comprehend him.

When the prodigals came home, we were just concluding a rather depressing meal. Look at them. Spence sputtered. I said I would, "Didn't I tell you?" They had actually gone to a bar and were severely injured. I responded, "All right, so what are you going to do now?" He cryptically replied, "Well, I don't know." Gable and Fleming were being persistently upbeat as we passed their table. After giving them a very stern nod, Spence bolted as I halted to scream at them. He was gone when I chased after him. For God's sake, we've got to find him, I said when I contacted Shirley. It's imperative that we contact him right away to avoid a crisis. We searched every tavern and pub in and around Riverside, but we couldn't find him.

The next morning, he failed to report for duty. Everyone became insane and thought he had gone on a bender. They couldn't replace him since he had become so associated with the image. While communications buzzed between March Field and M-G-M, we were stranded on location unable to film without him. Benny Thau heard Victor sob, "My God, we've got a situation on our hands!" You certainly have, and you darn well deserve to have one too, I reasoned.

Spence casually walked onto the stage a few minutes before noon, wished everyone a cheery good morning, and then got to work. I stopped Gable and Fleming from approaching him in a hostile manner, pulled them aside, and yelled at them, "Haven't you morons done enough? You have no right to act in such a manner. He needs to exercise caution, you know. Where are you thinking? I actually set them out as Spence smugly worked. I still don't know where he had gone, but he had taken his revenge by causing them pain.

Spence and I never again collaborated on a project, but we remained friends. On occasion, the studio made the assumption that I could handle him when he caused them problems. When Benny Thau called from Hollywood saying, "Myrna, we're waiting to start Tracy's picture. He's there on a bender, holed up at the River House with his male nurse," we were both in New York. Examine your capabilities. I contacted Spence, who inquired "Where are you?" and I responded by providing the information. I ought not to have. He didn't take long to arrive at the door of my St. Regis unit. He had been drinking for days and was angry. He made his customary play for me, and at one point he was so emphatically enraged that he broke a coffee table with glass on top. He then became hostile. He added, poutingly,

"You don't have to worry about me any more." "I've discovered the woman I desire." I felt gratified but yet a little let down when he listed Katharine Hepburn's merits. As self-centered as it may sound, I relished knowing that Spence was rooting for me. When nothing is expected in return, it is very wonderful.

Spence was a decent but complicated individual with an independent spirit and Irish Catholic guilt. I never considered him to be such a devout Catholic, but it turns out that he was since he would never divorce his wife. I ran across him at the Beverly Hills Hotel, where he lived alone, years after he first told me about Katharine Hepburn. I had no idea how he lived at home, assuming he ever did. He didn't typically have one. Why don't you marry the girl, I questioned him. And after that, he said, "Well, because of Johnny." I knew Johnny, his kid. Despite being deaf, he regularly stopped by my sets because, according to Spence, I spoke so well that he could understand me.

"What do you mean 'because of Johnny'?" I asked. I lost it. That is not an excuse. Johnny has gone through a divorce and marriage. Naturally, things were different back then. We continued to exist in that chauvinistic society. Additionally, I don't believe Kate, as he called her, wanted to get married.

To capitalize on Test Pilot's popularity, they immediately included Clark and me in another image. I had a small, rather ordinary part as an aviatrix who was, as the title suggests, Too Hot to Handle. Gable was primarily responsible. He is fantastic and hilarious as the newsreel reporter who fabricates stories. But the whole affair was entertaining and a little risky. According to that image, Clark allegedly saved my life. He was supposed to cause a burning plane wreck and then save me from it. From a valve behind the cameras, they opened controlled fire, and Clark rushed over to take me out. "Come on, those gas tanks will blow any minute!" he cries. I respond, "What did you expect 'me to do, you clumsy jackass?" At this point, the controlled fire allegedly failed, but Clark continued to approach and dragged me from the aircraft as it caught fire. News sources said that I may have burned to death ten seconds later. Although the incident gained a lot of media, it could have just been for show. In photographs, you act in some very bizarre ways, yet everything happens so quickly and you are typically well-protected. I don't remember experiencing any intense heat, so I can't really say whether Clark truly saved me or not. Such was the influence of M-G-M's public relations team under Howard Strickling.

The demands of filmmaking in 1938 were dwarfed by global events. In fact, after England and France gave up Czechoslovakia to placate Hitler in Munich, I was certain that war would break out. It didn't take a genius to see that this was another step in Germany's war-making process, but instead, many chose to trust Neville Chamberlain's foolish claim that ceding the Sudetenland would guarantee "peace in our time." He must have known that they had given Hitler control of Central Europe's military. Mein Kampf had been read by me; obviously, not many others had. Hitler's book describes everything he's going to do, and trust me, he's going to do it, I kept saying. The majority of folks paid it no mind. Of course, Arthur did; he was a wise politician. Generally speaking, though, few wanted to face this very real threat of complete war, save from a kind of conversational anxiety, like talking about the weather.

One of our Hidden Valley guests, Madeleine Carroll, who is intelligent, successful, gorgeous, and an excellent cook, used to rent a home to us in Malibu. She offered me several fantastic recipes that I still have. The final week of September, when they sold out of Czechoslovakia, we were down there with a large group of visitors. Jan Masaryk, the Czech Minister in London, entered the conversation as I sat glued to the radio attempting to understand the fallout from Munich. After a day of unsuccessful negotiations with the British Cabinet, he finally gave his speech at four in the morning, London time. That voice, carried across the wires from London to Malibu, was a clear indication of the man's character and the state of the world. Since his father had practically established democracy in his country and served as its first president—a magnificent experiment thwarted by Munich—this man evidently valued his country above all else. He said, "This is the beginning of the end; the beginning of a terrible war." I sent a wire to this man I had never met, expressing to him my support and encouragement because of the anguish and rationality in his remarks.

Years later, Edward R. Murrow, who was at the time reporting from London for his impactful broadcasts, admitted to me that he had spent that fateful morning with Masaryk. After his speech, they went back to the Czech Embassy to cook something like a souffle because Jan enjoyed fine cuisine and found comfort in the kitchen. According to Ed, my wire arrived that morning before those of kings, presidents, and other heads of state.

Two days later, I received a response from London addressed to "Myrna Loy, Hollywood". It only read, "BLESS YOU." JANUARY MASARYK.

Making pictures continued, an exhausting requirement in a chaotic society. Vincent Lawrence, who, curiously enough, did so well with Test Pilot, co-wrote a poor bit of whimsy titled Lucky Night. The studio decided it would be a good idea to pair me up with Metro's current heartthrob Robert Taylor. On our first day on set, I played records, something we occasionally did to pass the time during the protracted intervals between takes. In fact, Joan Crawford hired a person specifically to run her phonograph. When Robert Taylor came over, I was enjoying some lovely Cuban music. He asked, "Do you have to play that seductive stuff all the time? The filthiest music I've ever heard is this. My first day with him was on that day. I muttered, "Oh, brother!"

He was a little stuffy, but we got along just fine—during the photo, at least; afterward, I didn't like him. In 1947, he joined the group of men who leaked information to the House Un-American Activities Committee by naming the identities of innocent people. Actually, he did behave somewhat slyly on Lucky Night. He was engaged to Barbara Stanwyck, who I've always adored, but for some reason he sought to create a small triangle by making her believe I was interested in him. Theresa was informed that nothing could have been further from the truth when Barbara's maid brought up this issue. Since she arrived in a limousine on the final day of filming and whisked him away to get married, I'm not sure Barbara believed her.

In The Rains Came, Marlene Dietrich, Kay Francis, Tallulah Bankhead, and other actors supported Lady Esketh. Roz Russell, who openly admitted that she wanted the role herself, continued advising me for months that it would be foolish of me to change my type for the role. When Darryl Zanuck requested to borrow me for that part, I was taken aback. At least at the beginning of my time at Warners, he had never really valued my skills and I had never really thought highly of him. I had no idea back then that he was capable of creating films with such emotional impact as Gentleman's Agreement, Pinky, or No Way Out, and he most definitely had no idea how I would develop. Naturally, given his expertise in writing, he always placed a premium on the quality of the stories. Oh, he understood it was a smart idea to sign Betty Grable, but he wasn't as worried about finding cars that suited a specific star's personality as M-G-M was. Over the years, he and his wife, Virginia, became friends with me; I would spend Sundays at their Malibu beach house, but he never stopped annoying me at work. In Hollywood, the social life was typically kept completely apart from everything else.

I'll never understand why Darryl snapped at me. Perhaps he was trying to explain why he had fired me from Warners after I had achieved success. Do not overlook that. A quarter of the way through The Rains Came, he called me up to his office and started in on me, so I assume he wasn't letting me off the hook. He questioned my understanding, but he was never detailed, and he gave no useful alternatives. Awful treatment of an actress, that. What do you mean, oh my God? I sighed. "Let's bring Clarence in. He is familiar with me. Darryl has also hired Metro director Clarence Brown to helm the film. Darryl yelled, "No." I do not want Clarence to be present. He continued his meaningless tirade as I prepared to leave. What do you want me to do, I inquired from the door. Show up for work, he commanded. There it was. Really, he never made any sense. It's possible that he was worried that Lady Esketh would end up being the vamp he'd created for me in Across the Pacific in 1926.

Clarence told me to "forget it" after we talked about it. Don't allow him to get you angry. The novel's author, Louis Bromfield, used to accompany us to the beach on those Santana weekends. I questioned his opinion of how I perceived his persona. He told me, "As far as I can see, everything looks beautiful." In fact, I believe this is your best performance to date. So I remained steadfast.

Despite Darryl's schemes, the movie was joyful. We affectionately referred to Nigel Bruce, who played my husband, as "Bunny." He and his wife lived in the English colony, which was an area we explored extensively. Arthur, who is actually partly English, liked that crowd. I did too.

The Maharani was played by Maria Ouspenskaya. Maria was a little, skeletal sack of bones but she was so sweet and lovely. And a woman of such accomplishment! Before moving to Hollywood, she performed with the Moscow Art Theatre in Russia, appeared on Broadway, and owned an acting studio. She was lost in the labyrinth of lights and cables outside the set when I first noticed her. You won't believe how chaotic it is—there are dangers everywhere. And there, dressed for a test in her costume, this small creature stood. Oh, my goodness, being barefoot is so much joy, she exclaimed. She merely adorned her beautiful, tiny feet with sparse chains of pearls. I swooped her up and carried her onto the set, warning her to be careful of nails and other objects.

I frequently collaborated with Clarence Brown. I had a lot of faith in him since he had a deft hand. Darryl attempted to break that up, but it was unsuccessful, and we simply carried on. Clarence said, "You know, people don't die with their eyes closed," during my death scene. Why not attempt passing away while keeping your eyes open? All you have to do is hold your breath. I held my breath while maintaining my gaze on a stationary item until I noticed stars and everything began to blend together. When he finally yelled, "Cut!" I was starting to turn a little blue. You'll do anything for a director you have faith in.

In that photograph, I had another close call. On the former 20th Century-Fox backlot, which is now home to numerous hotels and office buildings, they built an incredibly realistic Indian street. I traveled on horseback with Tyrone Power down that street to a temple, where the title's rains began. Being raised on a horse, I had no qualms about practicing my own riding, but when the rain stopped, my horse reared up, turned around, and started back up the street. He left there feeling even more lost due to all the stalls, hawkers, and noise and headed straight into the center of the studio. I still felt somewhat in control as we sped past tiny roads in between vacant sets, but when we arrived at the cobblestone courtyard in front of the commissary, let me tell you, I've never been so terrified in my entire life. It would have been over if he had dumped me there. I crouched down and held onto his bridle and mane. As afraid as I was, he dashed for the commissary, arrived at the stairs, and by God, halted.

They came running, all these wranglers and other people; they were going to save me. In a poke of a pig! I will always wonder why I wasn't thrown. Oh, there was a scandal after that! The individuals who provided those animals were typically reliable, but when they ran out of experienced horses, they secretly sent one who had never worked in a movie. That error caused heads to turn.

I immediately moved on to my next scene, a tender moment with Tyrone Power in the temple. Ty, poor Ty, seemed to be more unhappy than I was about my unexpected ride. He was insane because a wrangler had taken his horse to pursue me, preventing him from joining the rescue effort. Ty Power was one of the most kind-hearted people I've ever met. He was a truly divine guy who was astute and kind. For me, it just so happened to be a poor time. There were issues at home and Arthur was starting to get into serious trouble. Around me, I could feel my world disintegrating. I never brought it up to Ty because I didn't know him well enough at the time, but he sensed it and made it his mission to make me feel better. One morning when I arrived on the set, he walked over with a long-stemmed bird of paradise in a Coke bottle, bowed, and presented it to me. That embodied the small gestures he would make. I regret to inform you that although we were almost lovers, we weren't. Although he was married to that awful Frenchwoman, I still loved him.

He possessed a keen awareness of interpersonal relationships that was enhanced by a certain mysticism and spiritual dimension. His warm, deep eyes revealed it to you. When he performed that kind of role in The Razors Edge, it looked like the ideal casting. Ty did that. To divert my attention from other things, he used to create games for us to play on the set. He questioned, "If you weren't who you are, what would you like to be?"

I retorted, "I have no idea in the world." If you weren't Ty, what would you wish to be?

I'd like to be the wind so that I can be light and free and be wherever I want to be at any time, he said with a graceful sweeping motion of his hands. I could travel the globe, peer into people's windows, and experience their pleasures and tragedies. That's all I could think of when he passed away. I said to myself, "Well, all right, he's the wind."

In the summer of 1939, I had three weeks in between assignments, so Arthur and I boarded a ship for Europe. We were able to relax a little bit thanks to our trip, which was something I had hoped would happen. Even with fears of war, Arthur was, as usual, the perfect tour guide. Fear was present throughout Paris. Purple drapes were placed around the Place de la Concorde to symbolically denounce Germany's invasion of another country, as only the French can do. But as an army of supporters closed in, the war I believed to be inevitable looked strangely far away as we traveled to Sweden. The M-G-M official ushered me into the lounge where hundreds of reporters and photographers were waiting for a promised press conference, supported by roses and an adoring entourage. Hitler was on the warpath, so it looked absurd, but if I wanted to leave that airport unscathed, I had no choice but to do it. We had arrived at the time of the Midsummer festival. On Midsummer Night, it rained, so everyone congregated in a large hall to sip foamy mumma and waltz to "Black Rudolph." It was a joyous arrival in the country of my grandfather.

We took the train over to Norway and rented a car in Oslo to take us to the fjords, which are sea channels that carve out steep cliff faces and are dotted with small houses and cherry trees. We wound up at an inn with fireplaces blazing in enormous open hearths and brandy served in warmed snifters after driving far, far up into the mountains, shivering from height and cold air. When I went outdoors, I saw tenacious tiny blooms poking through the snow. We descended and traveled to Bergen by boat across the fjords. Oh, my God, that's pretty much in heaven. Grieg's music was barely audible in the hills. You anticipated discovering trolls beneath each and every bridge.

We took a hydroplane to Amsterdam, where we were hit by reality. We were greeted by a furious Paramount employee who asked, "You didn't go into Germany, did you?"
No, he was assured by Arthur, "we flew over it on our route to Sweden. Why?"

Don't you know you're in Mr. Hitler's little black book, the representative asked as she turned to face me. You're at the top of his prohibited list; he has removed your images. It appears that the Führer was made aware of my backing for an economic boycott of Nazi Germany as well as my open defense of German Jews when my cable to Masaryk was published in the London Times. Well, I thought my photos should absolutely be prohibited. Why am I supposed to be amusing the Third Reich? The top brass of M-G-M's parent business Loew's, Inc. had a different perspective. Later, the founder's son Arthur Loew, who oversaw foreign distribution, wrote me a letter. On the set, the company's foreign greeter came over to me. He confessed to me, "I've been carrying this letter around for a long time." I just haven't had the guts to tell you about it. I still don't, but I must, so please advise me on what to do.

The letter began out quite sweetly before warning me not to combine my "politics" and "career." I gave it to him again and said, "You know what you can do with this." "Yes, that's what I thought you'd say," he retorted. Oh, Lord, I still want to spit because of this. They tell me to stop because there is still money to be made in Germany while here I am fighting for the Jews. Despite being Jewish, Loew and many of the company's executives approved of this atrocity. Although unbelievable, it actually did happen.

We took a plane to London from Amsterdam. Fear pervaded London. That's how close it was—they were arranging sandbags in front of Claridge's. But if the Normandie had arrived in New York in July, you wouldn't have known it. Several film reporters met the boat because we had a sizable crew of movie personnel on board. While the others agreed to participate in interviews in the foreign film industry, I avoided them. The possibility of conflict was never raised, whether out of optimism or ignorance. However, my husband was preoccupied with other issues as Arthur warned that French films were challenging Hollywood's B product in Scandinavia. The person who greeted the boat, Minna Wallis, always remembered with a wry smile how meticulously he oversaw the unloading of the vintage wines we had brought from Beaune.

The executive producer at Warners, Hal Wallis, told reporters that they intended to make 26 quota pictures a year in their Teddington, United Kingdom, studio. The British producer Herbert Wilcox would pick up Anna Neagle, his future wife, in New York before flying straight back to Scotland to shoot Bonnie Prince Charlie for RKO. Elsa Lanchester announced they will return to England early in October to star in The Admirable Crichton for Paramount while on their way to join Charles Laughton in Hollywood. All of that, however, turned out to be purely academic; six weeks later, American film production in Europe essentially stopped. On September 1, 1939, Germany invaded Poland; two days later, the United Kingdom and France declared war on Germany.

For the time being, I went back to my regular routine. The day after we returned, filming for the third Thin Man began. Bill Powell, who was returning to work after a two-year battle with cancer, was waiting for me when I arrived bright and early. He had made it through it, and they had removed it. For his 90th birthday a few years ago, I called him. When we began Another Thin Man, he still appeared somewhat fragile, but he was refusing to give anything up. Bill was shocked to learn that Nick Charles, Jr., had been added to the script. He moaned, "Why do we want this kid?" He'll start kindergarten soon, then prep school, and finally college. How old will we be after that? Bill, who was just in his forties, was acutely aware of aging. I was shocked to see him with gray, almost white hair when I visited him in the hospital following his procedure. I had no idea he had been dying for it for so long. Even by his fictional wife, he truly didn't like the way he came across. He continued, "There's a facility down here that emits silver dust. "It blows through the window and into my hair."

The series' final Dashiell Hammett original story was Another Thin Man, which was written by the prolific husband-and-wife writing combination of Frances Goodrich and Albert Hackett. You realize I've never seen them at Metro? It's bad, but the authors were rarely present on set unless they were called in to rescue us. The fact that I didn't meet the Hacketts until I relocated to New York in the 1950s suggests there weren't any issues. I'm glad to add that we grew close, and one day Albert jokingly explained why they didn't write the final three Thin Man films: "Finally I just puked on my typewriter. I was unable to write another one and could not attempt it again. These latter three barely impacted the prior ones, so perhaps we all should have agreed.

I went to Montana with Mother when I finished Another Thin Man. To say goodbye to us, Arthur made a point of arriving at the train. He wanted to eliminate any hints of strife that had been reported, even though they weren't wholly false. I wasn't abandoning him at the moment; rather, I was just eager to return home for the first time since we had gone after my father passed away. I didn't like how much of a state visit it turned out to be. The studio brought along Larry Barbier, my guardian, and a photographer in order to gain some notoriety from the event. Numerous local interviews were conducted. Official welcomes were given by the mayor and the Marlow Theater, where I made my dancing debut in 1917.

I was able to schedule time with friends, family, and a trip to the ranch. The split-log structures from Grandfather's farm and Grandmother's orchard were still there, but everything appeared closer together and farther apart. Remember, your legs are longer now than they were then, Uncle Elmer said. You no longer hold the things you once held in high regard.

Uncle Elmer, a charming elder man and a wild young man, usually had a funny remark. Twenty years later, when they hauled him to Hollywood and pulled This Is Your Life on me, he stole the show with his fascinating anecdotes about the good ol' days in Montana.

People appeared to be largely how I recalled them. Naturally, at first people watch every action you make closely, expecting to see terrible alterations brought on by celebrities. When they admit they can't locate any and regain your trust, it's amazing. They never questioned my memory of past occurrences when we were talking about them. They assumed that I would, and I typically did. Someone would comment how my beloved wild flowers were starting to blossom, while another person would make my favorite dessert. These were common knowledge that nobody questioned and that time could not alter.

I couldn't help but think of the Scandinavians I'd seen leading comparable lives but who were now in some manner under Hitler's control. Where were all those tranquil folks, living so happily? Our way of life is so excellent, I reasoned, that we should all be content as kings and prepared to battle tooth and nail to defend it. I used to advocate for war.

I went back to Metro expecting to get the job I'd been dying for: the Roman senator's wife who seduces Hannibal in The Road to Rome. It was slated to be produced with Clark Gable playing Hannibal, according to Joe Mankiewicz. One of the funniest scripts I've ever read was based on Bob Sherwood's adaptation of his play. I'll always cherish the scene where Hannibal displays a magnificent collection of keys to her and declares, in essence, "They are the keys to the towns I have conquered. What use are they right now? He wasn't portrayed as a tremendous military hero, but rather as a sincere individual who regrets the use of his life. The issue was that. It bemoaned the fact that half the world was at war. Joe reasoned that the entertainment sector would have a major influence on public morale if we were to join the war. It is apparent that in 1940, a script describing the absurdity of war lost its humor. We stopped generating. I've always felt bad about that.

Instead, they gave me the Bill Powell film I Love You Again. Despite not being Road to Rome, it ended up being one of our best comedies about marriage because of a sharp storyline and superb directing by Woody Van Dyke. Bill experienced some humorous incidents, such as a Boy Scout hike that still makes me laugh uncontrollably. After a terrible time following Jean's passing and his battle with cancer, he was back in top condition. A young Metro player named Diana Lewis had hit the scene. He took her to my place so I could see her, though it wouldn't have mattered because he was enraged by her. I hosted a dinner party and invited others we had in common, including Ronald Colman and Reggie Gardiner. She was cute, attractive, and charming, and Bill called her "Mousie," although she was 26 years his junior. We all had the right amount of skepticism and believed that a marriage would never endure. She was a beautiful wife to him, and their relationship lasted for more than forty years, until his death.

I made a change by using the left hand's third finger. I generally complemented the male lead, who usually carried the plot, with my photographs. This frequently implied that my roles were secondary, but that was exactly how I wanted it. Both the Bette Davis-style traditional woman's role and the Roz Russell female CEO routine, which I performed in Third Finger, Left Hand, weren't for me. It was Melvyn Douglas who got me through that. Theresa, my maid, and I both adored him; while she liked Bill Powell, Mel was her true love. People were drawn to his kind of friendly attentiveness. He was a wonderful man and an ardent supporter of liberal ideals. In fact, after Mel was made a lieutenant colonel in the California National Guard, certain American Legion factions began shouting "Communist" during the taking of the photograph. Don't assume that Joe McCarthy was the cause of all the panic.

In 1940, Humphrey Bogart, Fredric March, Jimmy Cagney, and other actors were accused of being communists by Representative Martin Dies and his committee. All of these people were kind, liberal-minded individuals who thought critically and stood up for what they believed in. Mel and Helen Gahagan were labeled radicals by conservative forces because they gave to the Spanish Loyalists and provided holiday feasts for the kids of low-wage migrant laborers. You understand, for these crusaders to criticize Hollywood, it's always excellent publicity. In the past, I was extremely close to Mel and Helen, and I later backed her when she ran against Nixon for Congress. Together, we all made the right fight.

Show people are known for their generosity, so everyone banded together to fight an even larger enemy. In the Coconut Grove,

Hollywood gathered 1,000 people long before Pearl Harbor to raise $15,000 for Franco-British War Relief. I was one of the cigarette girls along with Merle Oberon, Claudette Colbert, Annabella, Maureen O'Sullivan, and Herbert Marshall, while an unusual chorus line comprised of Charles Laughton, Herbert Marshall, Laurence Olivier, Ronnie Colman, Ian Hunter, Charles Boyer, and Bill Powell sang "The Man on the Flying Trapeze." At a Buy-a-Bomber Benefit, Charles Boyer, Roz Russell, and I sold peanuts alongside Cary Grant. Among innumerable broadcasts for countless deserving causes, Ty Power, Sam Goldwyn, Carole and Clark, and I broadcast for Greek War Relief. $10,000 from a Lux Radio Theater broadcast was donated by Bill and me to the Red Cross. The English community in Hollywood came together and dispatched a fully furnished ambulance to the British Red Cross each week. In addition to donating an ambulance, Bob Montgomery traveled to England to operate it. Though it was still "over there," the war was getting closer.

Paris was invaded by the Germans on June 14, 1940. When the news broke over the radio, Arthur and I were once more at the Malibu beach house. Paris—it seemed unattainable. Soon after that unsettling incident, Gilbert Miller and Kitty arrived with Jerome Kern. Jerry spotted the piano that had been there through many winters of fog and sat down to perform a song that he and Oscar Hammerstein had just composed. We were all crying as Jerry played "The Last Time I Saw Paris" while we were gathered around that old wreck of an upright piano that reminded us of the cafe pianos you hear in Montmartre and on the Left Bank.

In November, I left Arthur. The toughest thing I've ever had to do is this right now. Of all the guys in my life, he was the one I loved the most, yet I couldn't live with him. Believe me when I say that this is not how I usually behave. I left him five times and kept returning back. Once I've made a choice, I not only stick with it, but also block out the alternatives from my thoughts. Self-criticism is counterproductive.

That first time, I left the house and everything inside, never intending to come back. We had accumulated quite a bit. The items we received for our wedding alone might have supplied several dealers; people in Hollywood give expensive things. Betty Black said, "There's so much silver, the sideboards moan. Arthur valued those things highly and thought of them as his gifts rather than ours. To me, it didn't matter. I just handed everything over to him and moved into a little, furnished home in the Hollywood Hills.

Walking away from a marriage that I had assumed would endure forever broke me. God knows we weren't hasty; we'd been courting and living together for four years previously. Without a doubt, I was in a state of stress, and the media didn't help. Even if you try to keep quiet about these matters, they find out. When word of our split spread, Louella Parsons was in New York for a personal presentation. She actually interrupted her performance to dictate a bulletin for her column right there, much to the joy of the audience. Imagine if your personal issues were discussed in that manner. I still find it difficult to talk about the ups and downs of my relationship with Arthur since I treasure my stepson and his family. In addition, he is Arthur's son.

Most people who knew Arthur, I believe, would agree that he merely made fun of you. He was rude to his friends, staff, and coworkers. He developed into a really unpleasant person who was maniacally meticulous. Everything needed to be flawless. That's generally the case for the majority of artists. In terms of my professional life, it's accurate, but not in terms of my personal life. He developed a fixation for it. I once observed him placing tiny pieces of tape beneath the figurines on the mantel to direct the maid's placement. After some time, you reach a point when nothing you do is ever appreciated. I suppose it took him a while to get me, but he did.

While many of our acquaintances were aware of this, they were exempt from its effects. He was mocked by Collie Young, who never took him seriously.

I've always wanted that talent. Billy Wilder might poke fun at Arthur's arrogance. Billy responded when someone inquired as to why I had eventually gone, "Well, she just got tired of watching him test the Burgundy for room temperature."

I hired a lawyer with the intention of initiating divorce proceedings, but I didn't do anything else after that. It wasn't easy for Arthur to let go. While questioning my pals about what I was doing and who I was with, he pursued me once more. After Natalie Visart got back from my cabin at Arrowhead, he kept bothering her. At Paramount, poor Nat's office was next to hers, so anytime she arrived or left, he would rush outside to question her. We would howl after she later told me about it.

I returned four months after I had left him. He had relocated to Cherokee Lane in Beverly Hills after selling our Hidden Valley home. I didn't care what his motivations were for making the purchase; it looked like we could start over there. Arthur made an attempt, acting once more as my tour guide and taking me to Mexico, where we'd always had a great time. We slept with friends in Mexico City on a hill close to Diego Rivera's home, where barefoot women carried earthen jugs of water. I slept in a hammock next to the shore at Taxco after we traveled along a dusty road there. Acapulco's sky was still filled with clouds of untamed flamingos, but now it is populated by wealthy people and luxurious hotels.

Bill and I quickly produced two more movies. Bill pretended to be crazy in Love Crazy, which capitalized on the success of I Love You Again, so I wouldn't divorce him. He was amusing as usual, but my contribution was mainly limited to being the stodgy woman who had to put up with him. About Shadow of the Thin Man, all I can remember is that Bill was right about Nick Charles, Jr. He had already left for military training. That ended up being the final film in the series that Woody Van Dyke oversaw. In 1943, he passed very suddenly, leaving a large vacuum in both his friend and director circles. He used to be one of Hollywood's best and most versatile directors, so it baffles me that he seems to be ignored now. They may not have started honoring him yet due to his versatility. Whoever conducts these assessments in the media seems to favor genre directors because it's simpler. They will eventually get to Woody, though.

I traveled to New York to, let's say, catch my breath because things were still extremely difficult at home. After working on De Mille's Reap the Wild Wind for nine months, Natalie Visart arrived in need of a break. In those days, she was the only fashion designer who dressed not only ladies but also men and animals. Nat had a taste of traveling with a movie star because I wasn't carrying my studio bodyguards. We both found Fifth Avenue's shops decorated for Christmas to be fascinating, but every time we stopped to look at a display and Nat turned to speak, there would be a large head staring at me. It wasn't until after supper that we realized the streets weren't that crowded and we could actually wander around. We would therefore go for our walk and window-shop every evening at seven.

I made the decision to see a plastic surgeon. Since women were then frequently wearing their hair up in various Empire styles, David Selznick used to chastise me for having big ears. Oh, Myrna, you'd look great with your hair up, but you've got to fix those ears, he'd add. I scheduled a visit under the name Marjorie Williams in the hopes that the doctor wouldn't know me. I know that sounds unbelievable, but at the time, my ego was quite small. I told him about the issue, and he responded, "Let's take some pictures and see what can be done." He took pictures of me from every angle imaginable, including the front, back, left, and right. He even got up on a chair to shoot down at me. He seemed unusually thorough, in my opinion. Finally, he said, "Well, Miss Loy, I've got your nose." That son of a gun had known about me all along and planned to profit greatly from it. These photos will be really helpful to me because I frequently receive requests for a "Myrna Loy nose," he said. Therefore, I shouldn't have charged you for fixing your ears. I chuckled and promised to consider it, but I never returned. More pressing issues came up.

I was spending time with my stepson Terry the following afternoon, a Sunday, when his mother called. She exclaimed, "My God!" "They attacked us!" I learned about Pearl Harbor in that way. My buddy and fellow attorney Bill Sacks had arranged to take us out that evening. After the day's events, we weren't particularly in the mood for a night out, but we went nevertheless. The streets and bars in New York were filled with insane revelers. We met Robert Youngs somewhere along the way and spent the entire night together. Everyone appeared to be having a ghastly New Year's Eve because they were all in such an emotional condition and horrified. The following evening, we had intended to see the Youngs once more, but I got upset because I was concerned about Arthur and my relatives on the vulnerable West Coast. I told Bob, "I can't possibly come." I have to return.

In Burbank, you couldn't see the airport as we landed. Hollywood brilliance allowed them to entirely conceal it in the short time that had passed since Pearl Harbor. The studios contributed their talent and tools to transform the airport into a bland jumble of greens and yellows. There, Arthur came to meet me, full of news. His home was littered with tin helmets, sand buckets, and other accouterments of his new profession because he had become an air-raid warden. A Brooklyn-based anti-aircraft cannon was placed directly above us on the hill. They continued saying, "We're freezing to death in California," so I sent a heater to warm them up. It seemed amazing. In forty-eight hours, our world had altered.

Very quickly, everything started to move. Everyone was working on something. Hollywood was full of groups, titles, and passion. I was invited by Clark Gable to work in the Hollywood Victory Committee's Screen Actors Division, coordinating talent for hospital tours, bond rallies, and camp shows. Our division of fifteen was presided over by Clark, and on December 22, 1941, when the division met for the first time, Carole was the first to stand and proudly support her husband. Nobody could have predicted that Carole would perish in an aircraft crash three weeks later after returning from a bond-selling event. The only other Metro actors who were invited to Clark's modest private burial were Bill Powell, Spence, and I. Beyond consolation, Clark would only speak to Madalynne Fields, Carole's close friend and manager. Regardless of who it was, he refused to speak to anyone else.

Losing Carole, who was essentially Hollywood's first wartime fatality, grieved us all and fueled our will to fight. I put on a uniform for the Bundles for Bluejackets Hollywood Chapter and worked the night shift with Kay Francis at the Naval Auxiliary Canteen in Long

Beach. Kay belonged to a group of pals from Arthur's prior marriage who continued to hang out with him even after I entered the picture. Others were George Fitzmaurice and Edmund Lowe. They were all well-educated, Kay especially. She used four-letter terms that horrified me since she was a little ahead of her time, but I still liked her. While serving coffee and donuts to draftees headed for Hawaii in Long Beach, we shared a reality that went beyond titles and organizations. We witnessed the enlistment of untrained children who were all so young and confused and wholly unfit for war. It left us heartbroken.

One night, our military advisor informed us that we were on yellow alert. Prepare to close up shop and leave by eleven o'clock. Which we quickly did. Everyone responded violently at the slightest provocation after a Japanese submarine had shelled an oil field close to Santa Barbara. We were trying to make our way home in a state of near panic as we passed what is now Los Angeles International Airport. Then Howard Hughes and other aviators used it as a private landing area. The sight of dozens of planes lined up menacingly in the pitch black, their propellers barely moving, waiting for something to happen, is something I will never forget.

Before all hell broke out, I had hardly arrived at home. It sounded as though the world was ending. The Brooklyn boys were firing when I peaked out from behind the heavy curtains. The sky was littered with artillery fire, flares, and spotlights. In a hurry, Arthur, who had been sleeping, rushed downstairs. When I finally reached my family, Mother was in a fit of hysteria. "Take it easy," I advised. "Everyone is fine," which proved to be accurate. We had been in the infamous 1942 fake air raid, which no one has ever really attempted to explain.

After Pearl Harbor, I focused all of my attention on the war effort and the dwindling chance of keeping my marriage together.

At the studio, there was nothing but froth ready for me, and I wasn't in the mood for froth. That occurs occasionally. There won't be anything for a while after working like a dog for several months. A picture needed a lot of time to get ready for production.

Although I was heavily involved in both, I still went to the studio to shoot promotional reels for the War Bond drives and Bundles for Britain. One late night, while working on a pitch for a good cause, Lionel Barrymore said, "Jack's out in the car; I'm sure he'd like to see you. Why don't you go out and introduce yourself? God! He didn't recognize me from a hole in the ground when I went outside. It was terrible. The legend, who I had first seen walking down the hallway at Warners, was now sitting in the rear seat of a limousine, gray and battered, evidently long dead. What is said about the insulting effects of alcohol on the brain? He died two months later.

I was a complete mess at the time. It became clear to me that Arthur could never change, whatever of his desires. He worried that if everything and everyone in his immediate environment weren't perfect, it would reflect poorly on him and make him appear less than perfect. There ought to be a medical label for that phobia; I'm not sure whether there is. In a way, Arthur gradually understood that. Collier Young informed me after I had left, "He's finally seeing an analyst, but he won't lie down; he's walking around." Perhaps instead of attempting to be the ideal wife he desired, I should have given him a few good kicks in the teeth. I find it odd that I've never wed a man like my father. My husbands tended to be more controlling and shrewd than my mother, and I always caved in to them. Arthur was unreasonable in his demands. Terry, his son, was expected to excel in everything and win every competition. He once competed in a race against Bernie, our laundress's kid. When Bernie won, Arthur fought with Terry and harassed him mercilessly. He turned into a despot who imposed his skewed idea of perfection on us. You shouldn't treat people that way. It simply isn't that significant. Without a doubt, it is not significant enough to eliminate someone. Because I experienced it myself and then witnessed it happening to my stepson, it nearly ruined me.

The realization that you don't get along with one of your parents is painful, as Terry, Arthur's son and current Dr. John T. Hornblow of Farmington, Connecticut, and Watch Hill, Rhode Island, explains. It's difficult to talk about that. Every time I made an effort to build a relationship with him, I was rejected. He just genuinely didn't want a child, but oddly, he made up for it by being reliable, making the necessary payments, and writing the required letters—basically, by doing everything a parent should do except for the one essential thing: relating to the child and letting the child relate to him. With the exception of the rare handshake when I came or left, he never physically touched me. We met in a manner consistent with an appointment. Everything had a plan. Myrna was able to smooth off some of those edges while they were still married. She would occasionally bring me to the studio and engage in all kinds of impromptu activities with me, partially counteracting his coldness with her warmth.

He was the best at using his tongue to slash and cut while sitting behind his desk, and he did it without shouting. He was extremely good; someone should play him. He could inspire panic in someone who was weak, whether it was a child, a lady, or an employee. I'm not exaggerating. One time the terror was so incapacitating that I peed my trousers.

He was unpredictable when it came to his temper, either with Myrna or with myself. He once requested Swiss chard at a Hidden Valley luncheon, but none was delivered. He asked, "Where's the Swiss chard?" He was informed by Myrna that the market was empty. He chastised her in front of the guests, "I know there is some," he persisted. He abruptly ended the luncheon, asked everyone to return to the living room for more drinks, and left in search of Swiss chard. Lunch continued after it had been ordered and properly prepared. There was no way anyone was extremely hungry.

Another time, he ordered that no one in the house talk to me for a week after I had amassed enough black points in the book he used to track my daily offenses. One day, Myrna passed me in the hallway as she was about to say something but stopped herself. I can actually remember her eyes getting scared. She raised that lovely nose and went on her way. That punishment was probably just as difficult for her as it was for me. But I believe she was also terrified.

John Hertz, Jr. attended a dinner gathering at our home just before I said my final goodbyes to Arthur. He was a clever, attractive, and incredibly attentive advertising executive from New York, the son of one of the wealthiest men in the country. He grasped my hands in his during dinner. He said to me, "Your hands are cold and sweaty, but you are the beloved of millions." Without a doubt, Arthur had driven me to this point. I was a nervous wreck who looked like I was in danger. John got to work on that right away. I didn't consider the possibility that I might be stepping into hot water.

Printed in Great Britain
by Amazon